Flying The
Helicopter

Flying The Helicopter

by John J. McDonald

TAB BOOKS Inc.
Blue Ridge Summit, PA 17214

FIRST EDITION

FOURTH PRINTING

Printed in the United States of America

Reproduction or publication of the content in any manner, without express per-
mission of the publisher, is prohibited. No liability is assumed with respect to
the use of the information herein.

Library of Congress Cataloging in Publication Data

McDonald, John J.
    Flying the helicopter.

    Includes index.
    1. Helicopters—Piloting.   I. Title.
TL716.5.M36   629.132′5252   81-9196
ISBN 0-8306-2326-4 (pbk.)   AACR2

Photo Cover courtesy of Paul Garrison

Contents

Dedication

To all the unnamed and unheralded inventors who, working with make-shift parts in primitive workshops, made a reality of rotary-wing flight.

Acknowledgment

No book on any subject as complex and diversified as the helicopter could ever be the work of just one person. This book is certainly no exception. This work was possible only because of the help of my many friends in the industry. Because of them, many of the world's leading manufacturers of helicopters saw merit in this endeavor and most generously contributed information, illustrations, photographs, technical data, advice and review. Most importantly are these friends and companies who gave me their time and encouragement. It is now my privilege to thank them publicly and acknowledge their contributions. Whatever merit there is in this work is due to their unselfish efforts.

Kristy Whitsitt and Bell Helicopters Textron
Madelyn Bush and Boeing Vertol Company
Paul L. Shultz and Enstrom Helicopter Corporation
Bob Merzoian, Jr. and Hiller Aviation Company
David E. Wright and Hughes Helicopter Company
Karen Walling and Robinson Helicopter Company
John J. Fetsko and Spitfire Helicopter Co., Ltd.
And most of all Roman J. Biesiadecki, my research genius, illustrator and best of all friend.

Introduction

Since the dawn of time, man has dreamed of soaring like birds in the heavens and beyond to the unlimited depths of outer space. Long before man had traveled to the outer limits of his land-locked boundaries, and invented the boats that would carry him across the seas to distant lands, he was obsessed with the idea of flying. The concept that he believed he could fly is as old as recorded time itself. No one really knows just how far back in time it was that man first pursued this idea, this dream of flying. As we today venture out into outer space it is easy to imagine how and why our earliest ancestors sought to be stripped of their earthbound limitations and soar, as do the birds. It is that innate drive to reach for the stars that has given rise to mankind's finest hours.

First came toys, models that would soar up into the sky far above the fascinated crowds gathered to watch some crank display his idotic ideas that man could fly. At first these toys or models were crude and embodied hardly any of the principles of aerodynamics. As time went on, certain concepts, ideas, and designs began to appear and reappear over and over again. *Man was learning*. Learning about lift, wind, and thousands of other essential elements that, when put together with newer ideas, would allow him to fly.

They worked alone, ridiculed and scorned for who knows how many centuries. As discouraging as it must have been, their desire and drive only intensified. They gave their time, their money, and even their lives. They paid the price. And then, after what must have seemed an eternity, that glorious day came and man took to the air and flew for the first time. The conquest had finally begun. Balloon flight, glider flight, and finally the first powered flight. The world would soon be aviation crazy, making heros out of its pioneers, and legends out of its daring adventurers.

It is among the ironies of science that some of the first flight toys that flew were rotary-wing models. Yet these same rotary-wing aircraft (helicopters) would be among the later ways that we would use to conquer the skies. Once it began, it spread like a wildfire in the wind. No form of flight ever captured the imagination as did the helicopter. People to this very day will stand and look skyward to watch them fly in their distinctive manner: forwards, backwards, sideways, hovering over a single spot. No tool of modern man has so taken the world with its multitude of uses as has the rotary-wing aircraft. When some type of difficult but necessary flight is needed into some inaccessible place or terrain, or some almost impossible flight pattern in required, the cry you hear is *get a helicopter* . . .

John J. McDonald

Chapter 1

The Helicopter, A Brief History

The story of the helicopter is as long as it is fascinating. It dates back some 5000 years to a recorded beginning in ancient China, where so many sciences have first seen the light of day. The helicopter, or rotary-wing aircraft, as it is more properly known, finds its origin dating back farther than probably any other form of flight. Since the beginning it has been far slower in development than its younger cousin, the fixed-wing.

Both have beginnings in the form of toys and/or models. The dates for the first successful powered flight carrying man in fixed and rotary-wing aircraft were only four years apart. The evolution from this point on was won clearly by fixed-wing aircraft until the end of World War II. Since that time, the helicopter has enjoyed an evolution that can be matched by very few industries. It has proven to be the answer to numerous problems of travel, search, rescue, and industrial service. The helicopter has become, since its real beginning in the mid-1940s one of the most valuable tools of the post World War II era.

Early Development

There is documented proof of early attempts at rotary-wing flight as far back as 5000 years. In ancient China, somewhere around 3000 B.C., there appeared a toy called a Chinese top. While there may be considerable doubt as to whether or not the inventors were actually consciously taking the first step towards manned flight, they certainly did establish the basis for this type of flight. More than that, they made a major contribution in that they discovered, knowingly or unknowingly, the principle of *lift*.

Their little toy did actually lift and work on the principles which later became the foundation of a science that led to the development of not only rotary-wing flying machines, but flight in general. The Chinese top was a simple yet aerodynamically sound device, consisting of a stick with a simple propeller attached to it. The stick was spun between the hands of the user, and it would fly out of the hands, rise a short distance, and then in an autorotational manner fall to the ground (Fig. 1-1).

Leonardo da Vinci

There were in ensuing years and centuries many such devices, including paper rotary-wing toys capable of being thrown into the air and then autorotated down to the ground. The first real advancement in man's knowledge of this type of flight came in the 15th century, with the genius of Leonardo da Vinci. Leonardo was more than just a mere genius, he was a dreamer and visionary of things that would come long after his own time on this earth. He was the great inquisitor and observer. His mind could not stop, for he knew that there was not enough time in his lifetime to do, see, and try all the things that he would wish. Fortunately for all who would come after him, he would write in his journals, in mirrored

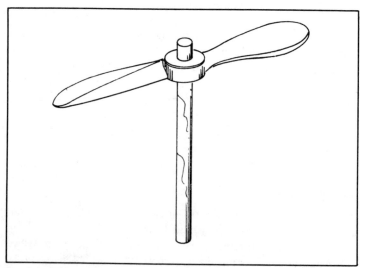

Fig. 1-1. Chinese top, circa 3000 BC.

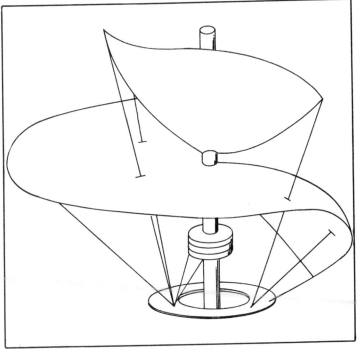

Fig. 1-2. Leonardo da Vinci's helix, circa 1483.

style, all that he observed and accomplished. One such observation, calculation, and hypothesis was on rotary-wing flight. da Vinci examined the principles of flight, lift, and control then designed and built an aircraft to experiment with. His experiments were doomed to failure before they began because he was thinking in terms of powered flight and no sufficient power plant existed at the time. Nevertheless, his contributions were such that he is today regarded as the "Father of the Helicopter." After a series of experiments, he theorized that air, itself, has substance (density), and therefore could be made to support a vehicle in flight just as it does the birds that fly. He hypothesized that when a bird flapped its wings on the downward stroke, they pushed down on the substance of the air (density), creating a lifting action for the bird. Next, he envisioned a giant screw that, when turned at a sufficient speed, would bore its way upward into the sky, just as a wood bit bores through a piece of wood (Fig. 1-2). This is known as *da Vinci's Helix*, and is the forerunner of the helicopter as we know it today. This was in the closing years of the fifteenth century and we cannot make too much of his contribution. Leonardo was the observer of the phenomena of science, the dreamer of tomorrow, and a leader of the Renaisance. Most of his life was spent as the tormented visionary whose contemporaries feared because they could neither compete with nor understand him.

The problems confronting all inventors with rotary-wing aircraft were three-fold: to keep engine and structural *weight* down to a point where it could lift itself and some useful payload; counteracting the rotor *torque* which would tend to rotate the craft itself; and to *control* the craft in flight. These problems would confound inventors for centuries to come.

The next significant advance in the evolution would not take place for over 200 years. It was at the World's Fair in Paris, in 1783, when two Frenchmen by the names of Launoy and Bienvenu demonstrated a toy they had developed. This toy was basically a stick, such as the Chinese top, but had four feathered propellers at opposite ends that turned independently of one another in opposite directions. This toy rotary-wing craft was powered by a bent bow system and was capable of soaring to heights of approximately 70 feet. This was the first demonstration of an answer to one of the fundamental problems of design: how to overcome the torque created by the rotor blade which caused the craft itself to rotate instead of the blades. What Launoy and Binevenu had accomplished was to invent the first true rotary-wing toy. Later came improvements utilized rubberbands for more efficient power, and numerous demonstrations were made, creating a sensation at the Fair. Representatives from many countries sent home descriptions of the little craft and inventors all over the world began working on the concept. It was logically reasoned that if such a device were successful as a toy, then why couldn't a model be built to carry man aloft? The urge to develop such a vehicle was born with many would-be inventors..It was doubtful that any one of these inventors would have believed that it would be nearly a century and half before their dreams would become a practical reality.

The Nineteenth Century

In the early 1800s, Sir George Cayley, an Englishman, developed a number of small model helicopters powered first by elastic substances, such as whale bone, and later by clock springs. Some of his models soared upwards into the sky nearly 90 feet. Finally, in 1862, he unveiled the first model ever to feature a fuselage. It was equipped with two booms, each with a set of rotors to provide the lift. Power was supplied by a small steam engine.

The weight of the engine, however, was too great and the craft failed to get off the ground. In spite of this failure, the craft had many unique design features that would be incorporated by others who would succeed.

At the same time as Cayley (1862) was developing his elastic powered craft in England, a Frenchman named Ponton D'Amecourt was developing a steam powered helicopter. While D'Amecourt met with very little more success than did Cayley, he did get far enough to prove a few principles and stimulate even more interest in the helicopter. His design incorporated contrarotating wings on the same axis, and of a coaxial design. The power was steam, but in a most unique design. The engine was made of aluminum and weighed only about four pounds. This, in itself, was an amazing accomplishment for 1862. However, the power developed was still not great enough to produce liftoff of the craft because of the power-to-weight ratio. D'Amecourt's craft was just close enough to the minimum power-to-weight ratio that it did stand on the ground and attempt to lift, bobbling from side-to-side as full power was employed. There was *just enough* action to prove the lift theory of the contrarotating wing. This was all the encouragement the world of inventors and would-be fliers needed to continue. Every day more and more inventors and scientists were turning their efforts to the task of flying and rotary flight in particular. An ever-increasing number of people were attempting flight and submitting designs for patents in most of the major countries throughout the world (Fig. 1-3).

By 1870, inventors from just about every major western nation were busy at work trying to develop the first successful rotary flying machine. Armed with the knowledge already gained from the work of such previous inventors as da Vinci, Cayley, Launoy, Bienvenu, and D'Amecourt, they pursued the problem with a new zest.

It was at this time that an Italian engineer named Enrico Foranini developed and built a coaxial steam powered helicopter. Foranini's craft incorporated a contrarotating rotor system. This unmanned ship weighed just six and one-half pounds. The rotor system was unique, consisting of a small diameter top rotor and a larger diameter bottom rotor affixed to the same drive system by use of a coaxial driven machine. The lower, larger diameter rotor was begun out at a distance beyond that which the top smaller diameter rotor reached. Thus, the air path for each rotor system was unobstructed by the air path for the other. By this un-

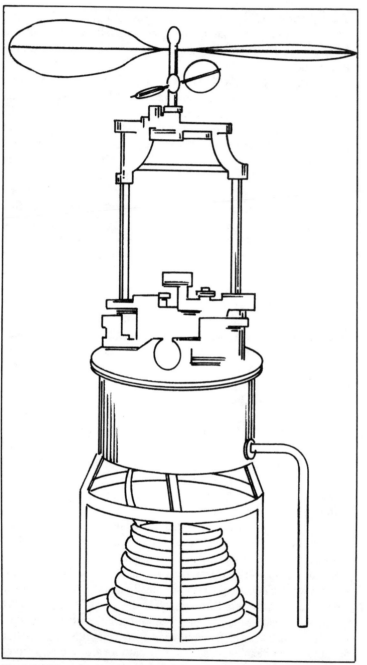

Fig. 1-3. D'Amecourt's coaxial, circa 1862.

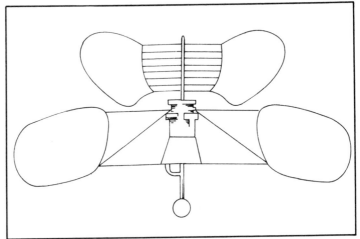
Fig. 1-4. Forlanini's steam helicopter, circa 1877.

obstructed air path to the individual contrarotating rotors, the ship would be able to utilize the rotor system more efficiently, especially during unpowered autorotational flight (Fig. 1-4).

Reports indicate that this steam powered model helicopter of Forlanini's rose to heights of 40 feet and remained aloft for as long as 20 minutes. This achievement only inspired the rest of the world's inventors even more. Rotary powered flight had been achieved, even though unmanned.

As the 1800's were drawing to a close, the whole world was becoming fascinated with the idea that man would soon be able to fly. Scientists everywhere no longer looked on the idea as insane, but rather were putting their expertise to work in an attempt to solve the remaining problems that hindered success. Much had been learned over the centuries, but much remained to be learned and done. Man's greatest achievement for centuries of effort had been a few minutes of uncontrolled powered flight by unmanned models. It is probably quite difficult for us to realize how this small achievement could have been so significant and inspire so many to contribute their work.

Some things had been learned that were of great importance. For example, a single overhead rotor had an effect on the fuselage, causing it to react uncontrollably due to the torque forces working against the fuselage. It became apparent to these early pioneers that what was lacking was a small, lightweight, high power-to-weight ratio power plant. Pneumatic engines had met with little or no success, the steam engine had achieved only a very marginal degree of success, and steam pods on the rotor tips had not been successful at all. The power plant seemed to be the major problem standing in the way of progress. "Give me an efficient power plant and I will give you a flyable rotary-wing aircraft" was the cry heard from these early pioneers.

There were, however, many problems that they had not even considered, or at least not given great thought to at that time. Among these were directional flight. Up to then, man had only considered lift and lift alone. No work seems to have been done on how, once in the air, you might move a craft in any horizontal direction. Lift, and *only* lift, was achieved. Directional flight would be a simple matter to work out—or so they *thought*.

There were problems with lift that they had not yet become aware of, but would be in the not too distant future. These were unequal lift and the forces known as *coriolis* (created by the effects of the earth's rotation). With the coming of the Twentieth Century, new names would be added to the list of inventors working on rotary-wing flight, and they would not only succeed in flying, but would overcome all of the problems beyond the expectations of even the most optimistic pioneers.

The Twentieth Century

Around the turn of the century, one of the great inventors of all time turned his energies to the problem of an efficient power plant. This problem was now in the hands of one of the most competent scientists of the day, Thomas Alva Edison. Unfortunately, Edison's experiments were destined to fail, though he had conceived an interesting concept that was to form the basis for much later and highly successful work by others. He utilized a solution of gun cotton impregnated onto a ticker tape, fed into a combustion chamber and fired by an electrical charge. What he had actually done was to develop one of the first internal combustion engines utilizing timed ignition and metered fuel injection systems. During his experiments, the gun cotton solution began to absorb heat from the engine and transmitted this heat back into the magazine where the impregnated ticker tape was stored for feeding into the engine. When the temperature of the gun cotton solution rose too high, there was an explosion resulting in extensive damage to Edison's lab. Edison never again returned to the development of an internal combustion engine.

By 1907, internal combustion engines had evolved which were beginning to develop the required power-to-weight ratio to make them practical for use in rotary-wing craft. Four years earlier, in 1903, the Wright brothers had utilized one in their successful first controlled power fixed-wing flight at Kitty Hawk, North Carolina.

It was at this time that a Frenchman named Paul Cornu was ready to test his helicopter. His design had dual rotors, one fore and one aft. The rotors were 20 feet in diameter and belt driven from a 24-horsepower internal combustion engine. Unique in his design were tilted vanes located below each rotor for control. Cornu took his massive ship out for testing and, seated at the controls, put full power to the rotors. The belts slipped badly, producing uneven revolutions of each of the rotors, and failed to transmit more than a small amount of power generated from the engine. Though all of these losses occurred and the lift was uneven, Cornu's ship lifted from the ground and *flew*! Though he only rose a few feet and remained aloft but a few seconds, Paul Cornu, in 1907, became the first man to achieve flight in a rotary-wing craft.

From this meager beginning would come others, and long before the Twentieth Century would be half over, true controlled directional flight, of a substantial nature, would be achieved. Mankind was on the threshold of success and rotary-wing flight was within reach. Activity increased rapidly now, and all over the world scientists were busy trying to overcome the remaining problems that stood between them and their goal.

In 1909, one of the men who would emerge as a giant of rotary-wing flight turned his attention to the problem. Igor Sikorsky, an obscure Russian aircraft designer, developed the first of many helicopters he would design and build. Sikorsky's ship incorporated a 25-horsepower internal combustion engine connected to twin 16 foot rotors, one above the other. The rotors were driven by concentric shafts, one revolving inside the other. Control was obtained by movable vanes mounted below the rotors. While his ship certainly was capable of lifting its own weight, there is some doubt as to whether it was able to lift itself off the ground with a pilot in it.

1910 brought a temporary end to Sikorsky's efforts with rotary-wing flight as he turned his energies to fixed-wing aircraft.

While Sikorsky's work was attracting little attention, a Frenchman named Louis Charles Brequet was testing a helicopter that was to affect rotary-wing design for the next 15 years. Brequet's ship was extremely large, utilizing four rotors. Each rotor was, in fact, a biplane wing. The four rotor design was an intriguing feature which captured inventor's imagination everywhere. Brequet's *heliplane*, as he called it, was barely more successful than Cornu's, it was able to provide only a few seconds of lift for the pilot and ship.

With the outbreak of World War I in Europe , some men naturally turned their experiments with the helicopter towards that effort. Two such men were Lt. Peroczy and Professor von Karman of Austria. They proposed that a helicopter be built to act as an observation platform. They were not interested in directional flight, but only that the craft could stay aloft with an observer over a single location. Their proposed design called for the use of three cables that would unwind as the craft ascended vertically into the sky. Their plan offered some merit, and they were allowed to construct their helicopter.

The ship itself, when built, utilized 10 foot contrarotating rotors powered by three 40 horsepower internal combustion engines. The cables were held taut during takeoff, but as the craft rose she exhibited great instability. In spite of this, numerous flights were made successfully. The ship, though remaining unmanned, rose to sufficient altitudes for the purpose and remained aloft for almost one hour.

While their ship never completed its task of carrying a man aloft as an observer, it did prove once and for all that adequate lift was possible in a rotary-wing aircraft. Petroczy and von Karman had proven what others had only dare dream before: the very concept of rotary-wing flight was sound. The only major problem that now remained was that of flight control of the helicopter. No one had even tackled the problem of trying to control a rotary-wing craft during flight. Even with just one problem remaining, it would be well into the 1930s before the first practical helicopter would be a reality.

The Final Phase

The intensity of effort to succeed now was moving at a tremendous pace. Designers of fixed-wing aircraft turned considerable attention to the effort of rotary-wing flight, as did scientists and inventors from almost every field of endeavor. The number of attempts and ships built between the 1920s and 1937 would fill a book more than twice this size. Only a few need mention here, though it should be remembered that every one of their efforts contributed knowledge and encouragement to the rest. In the final analysis, it is among these unheralded pioneers that real credit belongs for the unlimited success of the dream of rotary-wing flight.

Among the most noted of those working in this area were Emil Berliner and his son Henry. The elder Berliner had attracted considerable attention with his early helicopter models. Unfortunately, Emil died before his work reached a successful conclusion. His son Henry did, however, pick up where his father left off and designed and built two helicopters of his own. Between 1920 and 1922, Henry Berliner tested both of his ships and each is reported to have flown for several minutes. While they did achieve some momentary flight, they are said to have been highly unstable.

In the era from 1920 to 1923, the United States government got into the act by giving out the first governmental contract for the design and construction of a helicopter. This contract was issued through the U. S. Signal Corps to Dr. George de Bothezat. The ship he proposed featured four six-bladed rotors of 25 foot diameter, mounted at four individual points on the craft. The design emulated that of Brequet's in 1907.

The aircraft when completed was enormous, weighing some 3,400 pounds, and was sixty-five feet long and wide. The designer claimed a payload capacity of 1000 pounds. There were a series of auxiliary propellers and variable pitch main rotor blades used for flight control. In spite of its behemoth size and weight, the de Bothezat helicopter made several flights. During these flights, it displayed potentially good stability and control characteristics. The flights, however, were of one minute or less and at altitudes that never exceeded six feet.

Progress in France was also continuing at a rapid rate during this era. Etienne Oehmichen was developing the first of two interesting, if not totally successful, ships of rather complex and ingenious design. Oehmichen conceived a craft using a gas-filled balloon mounted on board along with two lifting rotors located front and rear. The aircraft proved to very unstable and almost completely uncontrollable, but it did manage to lift the machine and pilot.

After this somewhat successful achievement in 1920, Oehmichen was encouraged to design and build yet another ship. Finally, in 1924 he unveiled his second ship which featured four 21 to 25-foot rotors; again in the fashion of Brequet's 1907 machine. He added, in addition, five small horizontal propellers plus two propulsive and one steering propeller. This helicopter incorporated thirteen separate transmission systems and was powered by a 120-horsepower engine. This aircraft, which was ingenious in design in so many ways, made in excess of *one thousand flights*, each lasting several minutes. In spite of showing great promise, the obvious over-complexity of the craft made it completely impractical.

Meanwhile, the Spanish were not to be outdone, and Marquis de Pescara built and flew several ships in the period between 1920 and 1926. The greatest of the Spanish pioneers, most assuredly, was Juan de la Cierva. During the 1920 and 1924 era, he designed and built several fixed-wing aircraft. de la Cierva lost one of his ships and decided to investigate rotary-wing flight. His idea was to develop a craft that could land at a relatively slow speed. Soon he displayed his new type of aircraft, one that incorporated many of the features of a fixed-wing craft with a freely rotating overhead rotor system. He named this type of aircraft an *autogyro*.

The autogyro incorporated a conventional propeller to provide forward thrust, and the overhead rotor to provide lift. The larger overhead rotor was not power-driven but was merely allowed to windmill. It required a forward speed of only about 30 miles per hour to produce the required rpm of the rotor to provide the necessary lift (auto rotating). This early autogyro had a tendency to roll over on its side due to uneven lift forces. After a great deal of experimentation, he discovered that the advancing half of the rotor was traveling at a faster rate of speed than the retreating half. This is what we know as *dissymmetry of lift*.

Juan de la Cierva's solution to the problem was to employ flexible blades attached to the rotor hub by hinges. This permitted the advancing blades, which had more lift, rise, thereby reducing their effective lift area to that approximating the lift area of the retreating blades. His experimentation, explanation of the problem, and solution was one of the most significant contributions to the development of the helicopter as we know it today. This, along with his autogyro concept of the freely rotating rotor, showed the helicopter inventors and pilots how they might make emergency landings in case of a power failure.

In 1928, Juan de la Cierva was to receive the publicity and recognition due him. In that year he personally took one of his autogyros and crossed the English Channel; and did so at nearly 100 miles per hour. This flight convinced the world that the autogyro was a success, extremely safe, and fullproof because of its unique capabilities.

The Decade of Success

With the advent of the 1930s came a realization that a truly practical craft was at hand. With this new decade came the expectation that the reality of rotary-wing flight would be finally here.

First, there came an Italian named d'Ascanio with his helicopter that incorporated trim tabs to regulate the tip plane path of the rotor blades; then, the Dutchman von Baunhauer, who would be the first to utilize a single main rotor with a vertical tail rotor to compensate for torque. Also, Berquet, the Frenchman who had done so much earlier, built still another ship that showed promising flight characteristics but was destroyed before actual test data could be compiled.

In 1937 war clouds were hanging over Europe and designers everywhere were racing against the clock of ensuing disaster. Heinrick Focke, later to be regarded as one of Germany's greatest aircraft designers, achieved this sought-after goal: a practical helicopter. This ship, known as the Focke-Acheglis helicopter, was to be the one that would make rotary-wing flight after so long a practical reality. Between 1937 and 1939 it established many records, among the more important are:

Duration: 1 Hour, 20 minutes, 49 seconds.
Distance: 143.069 Miles in straight line flight.
Altitude: 11,243 Feet.
Speed: 76 Miles per hour.

What is just as interesting as the records set by the FW-61 (as it was officially designated) was a demonstration that was given with it in the *Dutchland Halle* in Berlin. First, the ship was piloted by a woman test pilot, Hanna Reitsch, which was quite an achievement for the 1930s. Inside this hall, which measured only 250 feet in length and 100 feet in width, she demonstrated forward, backward, and sideways flight. She also demonstrated the craft's ability to hover over a single spot and make 360 degree turns while remaining over that fixed spot.

The aircraft itself was equipped with two lateral booms onto which the main rotors were mounted. These rotors turned in opposite directions to compensate for torque. The aircraft was controlled by changing the pitch of the rotor blade. It was powered by a 160-horsepower engine which was cooled by a small wooden propeller mounted on the nose section. The entire craft weighed just 2,400 pounds (Fig. 1-5).

This was the beginning, and the development would proceed rapidly as the word and result of Focke's work spread throughout the world. In the United States, the Air Force, in 1940, accepted the Platt-Lepage helicopter for testing. This ship, while encouraging, lacked lateral stability; it was not accepted by the Air Force. In 1939, Igor Sikorsky resumed his work with helicopters and began the development of a new ship. Sikorsky, not chosing to follow Focke's lead and go with dual contrarotating rotor blades, went instead with the idea put forth by von Baunhauer, in 1930.

The Day of the Helicopter

On May 6, 1941, Sikorsky broke Focke's helicopter endurance record by almost 12 minutes. The day of the helicopter as an experimental craft was drawing to a close. The helicopter was about to come out in production and begin a development era possibly unmatched in the annals of industrial development. New names were appearing on the horizon—names like Lawrence D. Bell, founder of Bell Aircraft Company, who, on November 1, 1941, ordered the development of a Bell helicopter to begin. This was followed by the first successful flight of a Bell helicopter on July 29, 1943, and the first American indoor flight inside the 65th Regiment Armory in Buffalo, New York, on May 10, 1944. Finally, on March 8, 1946, Bell's model 47B was granted the world's first commercial helicopter license, then helicopter type certificate Number One was issued to Bell by Civil Aeronautics Administration.

These giants would shortly be joined by another giant and pioneer, aviator Howard Hughes. Hughes Aircraft Division designed and successfully flew a ship called the Flying Crane. This was a huge helicopter capable of lifting some four tons. In 1958, Hughes Tool Company, Aircraft Division, unveiled the first of many highly competitive helicopters such as the Hughes 269A. With this, Hughes Helicopters was born. The names to add to the list of pioneers and developers of the modern helicopter are legion; names such as Hiller, Spitfire, Boeing Vitrol, Enstram, and most recently Robinson. We will have more to say about their achievements in future chapters. But it is significant to point out that they all added to some degree to the betterment and safety of all who fly in those strange looking whirleybirds.

Introduction to the Future

The evolution of the helicopter begins anew every day in engineering offices all over the world. The inspiration for de-

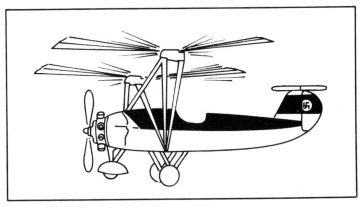

Fig. 1-5. Focke's dual rotor helicopter, 1937.

velopment comes to some extent from within, but possibly to an even greater extent from the sales forces who are constantly uncovering new needs and demands from potential customers wherever helicopters are flown, and perhaps more importantly, from where they aren't. Where the future development of the helicopter will lead, no one can possibly predict. But judging from the past it will astound, amaze and dazzle us all. I only hope that those pioneering men and women who made this dream of rotary-wing flight come true see the wonders that they and their toil have brought forth. If it is true that the future can be predicted by studying our past, then I, for one, can hardly wait.

Chapter 2

Fundamentals Of Aerodynamics

Before discussing the phase of aerodynamics which pertains to helicopters, let's review our basic theory of flight. We know that four major forces acting on any aircraft are *weight* (or gravity), the force acting downward; *lift*, the force acting upward; propulsive *thrust*, the force acting forward (or, in the case of the helicopter, in any direction); and *drag*, the retarding forces of inertia and air resistance acting opposite to propulsive thrust force. Lift opposes weight, and propulsive thrust opposes drag. Drag and weight are forces inherent in anything lifted from the earth and moved through the air. Thrust and lift are artificially created forces used to overcome the forces of nature and enable an aircraft to fly. Lift overcomes or balances gravity, depending on the condition of flight. Unlike the airplane, the helicopter obtains both lift and thrust from its main rotor system. In forward flight, propulsive thrust is forward and drag to the rear. In rearward flight, the two are reversed. In vertical ascent, thrust acts upward in a vertical direction while drag, the opposing force, acts vertically downward. In short, propulsive thrust acts in the direction of flight and drag acts in the opposite direction. Remember, we are dealing here with thrust and drag forces acting on the airframe, *not* with the forces within the rotor system (Fig. 2-1).

Bernoulli's Theorem

This is sometimes referred to as the *Venturi effect*. If the wall of the tube is narrower in one part than another, the air must travel

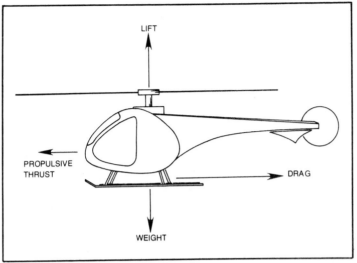

Fig. 2-1. Four forces acting on any aircraft.

faster in passing the narrow point because the same volume of air must pass this point as passes all other points (Fig. 2-2). It would be natural, of course, to assume that pressure is also greater in the narrowest point in the venturi tube, but this is not so. The increased air velocity actually brings about a *decrease* of pressure at the narrowed throat of the tube. It is this principle which enables an airfoil to produce the greater portion of the force we call lift. Now,

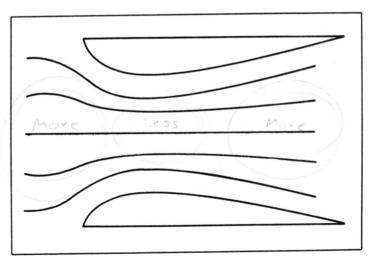

Fig. 2-2. Venturi effect.

compare the lower surface of the airfoil in Fig. 2-3 with the parallel walls on the venturi tube, and the upper surface of the airfoil to the curved profile of the constricted neck of the tube. One-half of the venturi tube is nothing more nor less than a section of an airfoil.

The Airfoil

An airfoil is any surface designed to produce lift when air passes over it (Fig. 2-4). The reason an airfoil produces lift is a differential in air pressure above and below it. Based on the Bernoulli theory, it follows that the faster-traveling air at the top of the airfoil will produce a lower pressure than exists on the bottom surface. On a conventional airplane, the wings are the airfoils.

On the helicopter, the rotor blades are the airfoils (Fig. 2-5). The same aerodynamic principles apply to all airfoils. On fixed-wing aircraft, lift is brought about by forward motion, whereas in the rotor-winged craft it is brought about by the rotor blades traveling in a circular motion.

Chord. The *chord* of an airfoil is an imaginary line connecting the leading edges and the trailing edges of the airfoil (Fig. 2-6).

Span. The *span* of the helicopter blade is the maximum distance from the root of the rotor blade to the tip, measured from the rotor centerline to the blade tip (Fig. 2-7).

Lift. *Lift* is a variable force. Many things govern the amount of lift received under stated conditions. Visualize this cross section of an airfoil either as a fixed wing or the rotor blade of a helicopter.

Angle of Attack. The *angle of attack*, that angle between the chordline of the airfoil and the relative wind (the oncoming wind flowing parallel and opposite to the flight path of the airfoil),

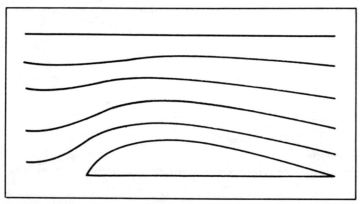

Fig. 2-3. Airfoil acts like one half of a venturi tube.

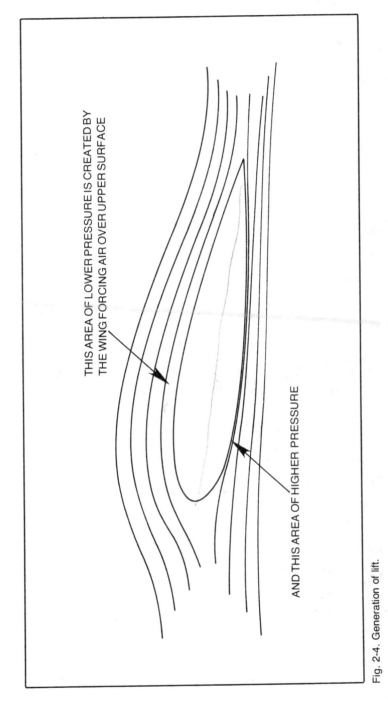

THIS AREA OF LOWER PRESSURE IS CREATED BY THE WING FORCING AIR OVER UPPER SURFACE

AND THIS AREA OF HIGHER PRESSURE

Fig. 2-4. Generation of lift.

27

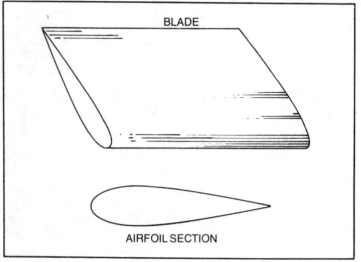

Fig. 2-5. Rotor blades have airfoil sections.

governs lift (Fig. 2-8). The greater the angle of attack, the greater the lift—this condition prevailing until the angle becomes so great that the flow of air over the top of the airfoil can no longer follow the camber smoothly, but is broken up and burbles. The airfoil is then fully or partially *stalled*, depending on the severity of the angle and the aerodynamic characteristics of the airfoil.

Velocity of Air. Lift demands a rapid flow of air over an airfoil before it becomes effective. The helicopter accomplishes this by rotating its airfoils through the air around the shaft, power

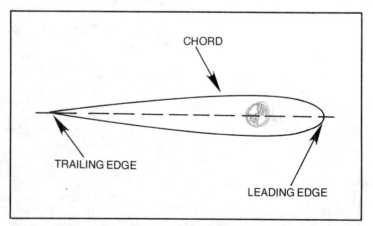

Fig. 2-6. The chord is an imaginary line between the leading and trailing edges.

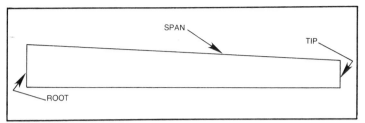

Fig. 2-7. Span is the distance from rotor to tip.

being derived from an engine driving the rotor shaft, or in some cases by tip-reaction-type engines. In the helicopter, lift is possible without any horizontal movement at all. The conventional airplane varies the airfoil angle of attack by changing the attitude of the entire aircraft. In contrast, the helicopter, as shown here, changes the airfoil angle of attack by varying the pitch of the main rotor blades without changing the attitude of the craft. In a helicopter, the airfoil angle of attack is developed throughout the complete cycle of 360 degrees by the rotation of the rotor system, and it usually varies considerably. This variation is dependent upon flight conditions. The high-speed rotatation of the rotor blades determines the direction of relative wind over the rotor blades.

Angle of Incidence. The angle of incidence is the angle formed by the chord of the airfoil and the longitudinal axis of the aircraft (Fig. 2-9). The conventional airplane's wing angle of incidence is built into the aircraft by the designer and cannot be changed by the pilot. The helicopter's blade angle of incidence can be changed at will by the pilot by changing the collective pitch of the motor blades. Like the angle of attack, the angle of incidence

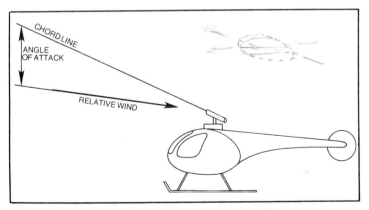

Fig. 2-8. Angle of attack is angle between chord line and relative wind.

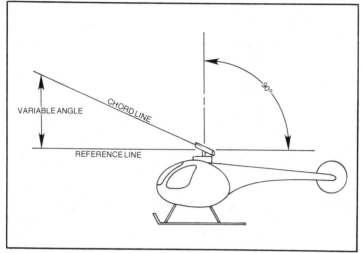

Fig. 2-9. Angle of incidence.

continually changes as the rotor revolves, whenever the control stick is moved from the neutral position and the rotor plane of rotation is tilted.

Resultant Lift. For the purpose of design, the forces acting on the airfoil are concentrated and acting through one point known as the *center of pressure*. On each tiny portion of the airfoil surface, there is a small force acting. This force is different in magnitude and direction from the force acting on other small areas of the surface farther forward or rearward. It is possible to add, mathematically, all of these forces, taking into account their magnitude, their direction, and their location. The sum of all the tiny forces over the surface of the airfoil is called the *resultant lift*. This resultant lift has *magnitude, direction*, and *location*. The point of intersection of the line of direction of the resultant with the chord is called the *center of pressure*, or CP. Normally, the center of pressure is located at a point approximately one quarter or 25 percent of the way back from the leading edge (Fig. 2-10).

Airfoil Configurations. Airfoil section configurations vary considerably. An airfoil may be *asymmetrical* or *symmetrical*, depending on the specific requirements to be met (Fig. 2-11).

Even though the airfoil is symmetrical and there is no greater curvature on its top surface than on its bottom surface, when it is inclined into the airstream, the path of air travel over the top of the airfoil is longer than the path under the airfoil (Fig. 2-12). The relative wind striking the airfoil on a lower point on the leading

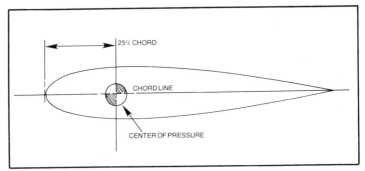

Fig. 2-10. Location of the center of pressure.

edge has to travel further following line A over the top surface than it does following line B on the bottom surface. Therefore, having to travel farther, it travels faster, resulting in a decreased pressure on the top side which, in turn, produces lift.

The blade tip velocities sometimes exceed 450 mph. Remember that drag increases as the square of the speed. For maximum efficiency of the entire blade, we would want an airfoil which is efficient at the relatively low speeds found at the root of the blade as well as the high speeds encountered at the tip.

Trim Tabs. Whenever a symmetrical airfoil developing lift has a trim tab that is to be utilized for blade tracking, the CP can be moved towards the trailing edge by bending the tab down. The tab bending causes a low-pressure area to be generated on the top side of the bend when bent downward and the reverse when bent upward. Excessive tab bending will cause a cyclic stick shake (Fig. 2-13).

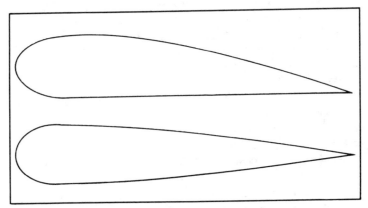

Fig. 2-11. Asymmetrical airfoil (top), symmetrical airfoil (bottom).

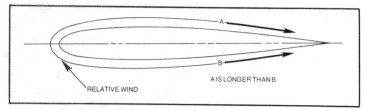

RELATIVE WIND

Fig. 2-12. Symmetrical airfoil in action.

Blade Twist and Stall. There are several rather unrelated but very important items that influence the hovering and vertical flight performance of rotors. One of these is *blade twist*. Rotor blades are generally built with a twist incorporated along the span. This achieves a more even distribution of lift over the entire blade. That part of the total induced loss arising from a nonuniformity of inflow may be minimized by twisting the blade so that its root end has a higher pitch angle than the tip (Fig. 2-14). The greatest angle of attack is at the root, decreasing at the center with the least angle of attack at the tip. Blade stalling is delayed when twist is employed because twist unloads the tips by reducing the tip angles of attack. Earlier designed blades were tapered as shown in the top view. The taper changed the area across the span, having a greater area at the root, decreasing towards the tip. When the constant chord design was adopted, blade twist was incorporated. The twist is allowed certain tolerances during manufacture. As a result of the twist tolerance, trim tabs were added to aerodynamically twist the blades in flight in order to have the blades generate the same amount of lift under a given condition. Tracking is an approach to obtaining the blade lift sharing desired.

Fixed Wing Versus Rotary Wing. The airplane depends on its wings for lift; the autogyro receives its lift from the freely rotated rotor blades and depends on forward motion created by an engine-driven propeller. The rotor blades of a helicopter are its wings, its propeller, speed and directional controls; thus, the helicopter is essentially a set of power-driven rotating wings which support a weight-carrying structure. There are a number of different types of rotor systems. We will discuss the fully articulated system. A rotor system of three or more blades that are individually hinged so that each blade has freedom of motion both up and down, fore and aft, and a change of pitch or rotation around the feathering axis is called a *fully articulated system* (Fig. 2-15).

Rotor Disc Area. As previously stated, lift is obtained by the rotating blades of the helicopter. The area swept by the rotating

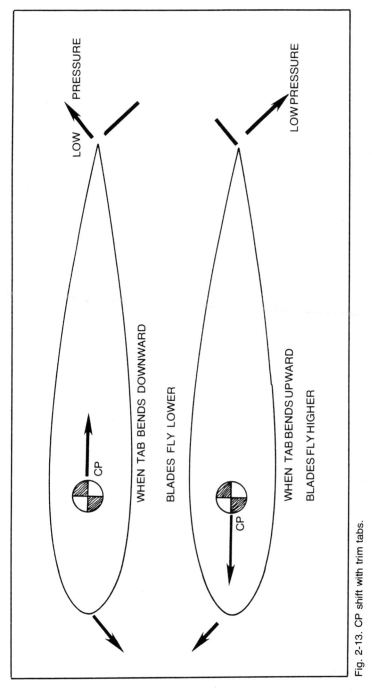

Fig. 2-13. CP shift with trim tabs.

LOW PRESSURE

WHEN TAB BENDS DOWNWARD

BLADES FLY LOWER

CP

LOW PRESSURE

WHEN TAB BENDS UPWARD

BLADES FLY HIGHER

CP

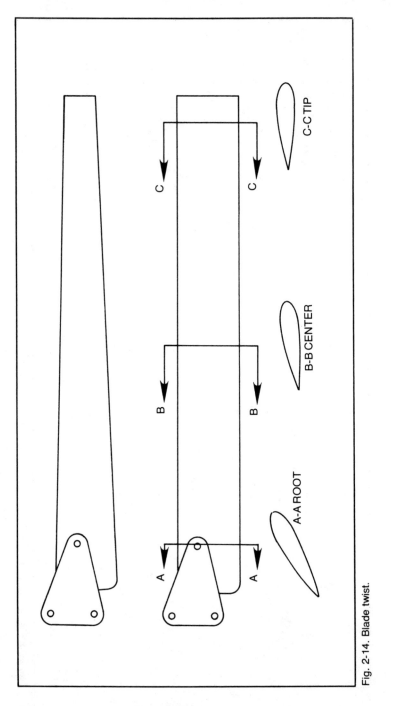

Fig. 2-14. Blade twist.

34

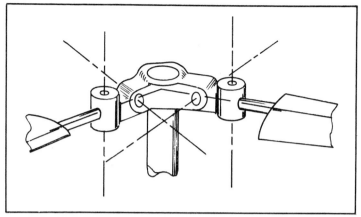

Fig. 2-15. Fully articulated rotor system.

blades in one revolution is theoretically a horizontal, circular area and is called the *disc area*. The rotor disc made by the blades in rotation can be seen if one can look down on the blades from above. The rotor disc would be the area of the circle made by the tips of the blades in rotation (Fig. 2-16).

Tip Path Plane. To a certain extent, conventional aircraft and helicopter aerodynamics in terms are similar; however, there are many new terms which the helicopter mechanic must understand. One of these is *tip path plane*—the path through the air in a circular motion made by the tips of a blade is known as the tip path plane. In other words, the tip path plane is the imaginary circular

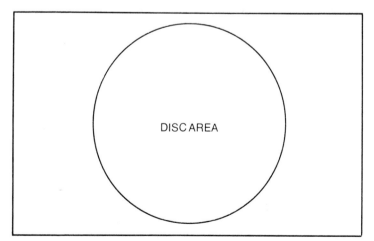

Fig. 2-16. Disc area (vertical view).

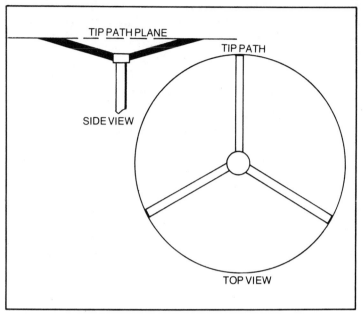

Fig. 2-17. Tip path plane.

surface formed by a plane passed through the average tip path of the rotor blades. If viewed from above, the tip path plane would appear as a circle, as shown on the left in Fig. 2-17. In rotation, the tip path plane has a visually solid appearance. In side view, one can easily see if there is any change of tilt in the path of the blades. Rotor disc has much the same meaning as tip path plane.

Tracking. The path subscribed by rotor blades during their cycle of rotation is known as *tracking*. It is important that the blade tips rotate in a common plane, much the same as the propeller of an airplane. The blades must track in approximately the same place, or a severe vertical vibration will result. If the tips are rotating in different planes, they are *out-of-track* (Fig. 2-18). The higher blade is generating more lift. The blades are *in track* when the tips are rotating in a common plane (Fig. 2-19). This generally causes all the blades to generate the same amount of lift under a given condition; however, the complete span of the blade should be considered when bending tabs for tracking.

Tracking through usage also denotes the mechanical procedure used to bring the blades into satisfactory flight conditions. Several methods of checking the track of blade tips are used. Figure 2-20 shows one method of tracking the main rotor blades. If

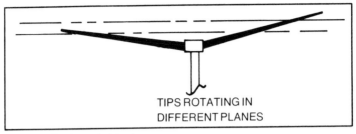

TIPS ROTATING IN
DIFFERENT PLANES

Fig. 2-18. Blades out of track.

found to be out-of-track, adjustments are made in the blade pitch mechanism and the trim tabs until all blades are again in track with each other.

Some helicopter blades have trim tabs made of metal and will cause the blade to fly higher or lower by bending the tab up or down. As previously stated, excessive tab bending can cause cyclic stick shake by moving the CP. As the tab is bent, it also increases the drag component of the blade (Fig. 2-21). Blades can be unequally spaced to the point where a lateral vibration can be noticed. This problem can usually be observed by the strobe reflective images being unequally spaced. Blade tracking must be approached by considering the drag component as well as the lift. The end product is to obtain the same amount of lift and drag on all blades for a smooth-flying helicopter.

Tail Rotor Tracking. Figure 2-22 illustrates a method of tracking the tail rotor blades. If all rotor blade tips follow precisely the same track, the possibility of blade vibration is minimized.

Thrust

During vertical ascent, thrust acts vertically upward while drag and weight act vertically downward (Fig. 2-23). Drag, oppos-

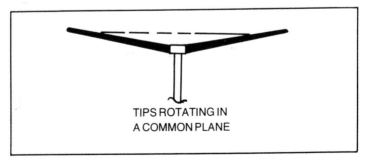

TIPS ROTATING IN
A COMMON PLANE

Fig. 2-19. Blades in track.

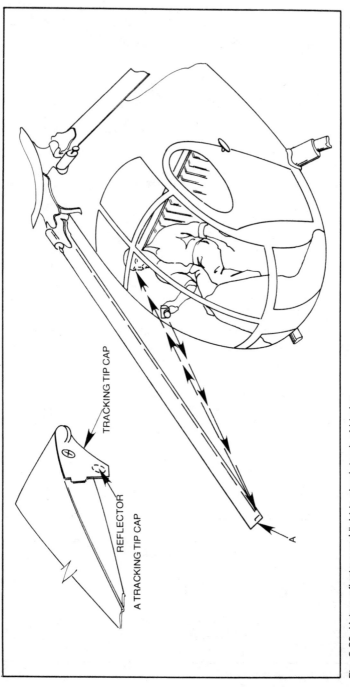

TRACKING TIP CAP

REFLECTOR

A TRACKING TIP CAP

A

Fig. 2-20. Using reflectors and light to check track of blades.

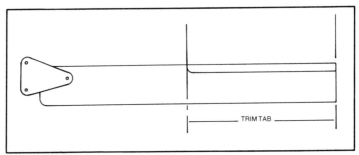

Fig. 2-21. Improper trim tab adjustment may cause tracking problems.

ing upward motion of the helicopter, will be increased from the downwash of air from the main rotor. Thrust must be sufficient to overcome both of these forces. The main rotor, as previously stated, is responsible for both propulsive thrust and lift; therefore, the force representing the total airfoil reaction to the air may be considered as two components. One component, *lift,* is the force required to support the weight of the helicopter. The other component, propulsive *thrust,* is the force required to overcome a drag on the fuselage (Fig. 2-24). During vertical ascent or hovering, the tip path plane is horizontal and the resultant force acts vertically upward.

Helicopter Control Systems

Directional Flight Force. A pilot accomplishes forward flight by tilting the tip path plane forward through cyclic pitch

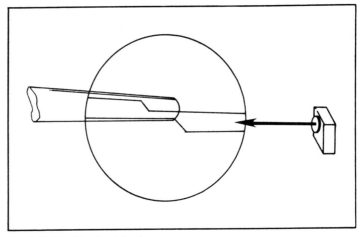

Fig. 2-22. Tracking the tail rotor.

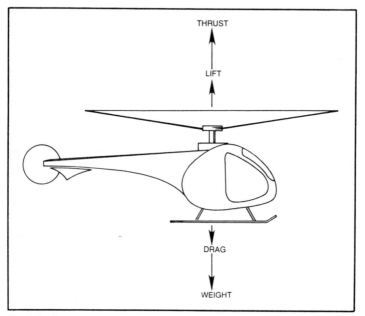

Fig. 2-23. During vertical ascent, thrust acts in same direction and in line with lift.

control. The total blade force tilts forward with the rotor total thrust acting both upward and forward. The component *lift* is opposite *weight*. The other component, propulsive *thrust*, acts in the direction of flight to move the helicopter forward.

In any kind of flight—forward (Fig. 2-25), vertical, hovering (Fig. 2-26), backward (Fig. 2-27), or sideward—the lift forces of a rotor system are perpendicular to the tip path plane or plane of rotation. Terms are often used interchangeably.

Lateral, Rolling, and Vertical Axes Control. The axes of the helicopter are the same as we know for the airplane. The lateral axis is an imaginary line running through the center of the aircraft from side to side; movement about this line being described as *pitch*, or the nose-up/nose-down movement. The longitudinal axis is an imaginary line through the center of an aircraft from nose to tail, with movement around this line being described as *rolling*. The vertical axis is an imaginary line running through the center of the aircraft perpendicular to the other two axes; movement about this axis being known as *yaw*, or nose-right or nose-left. To control completely the position and attitude of a body in space requires control of the forces and movements about all three axes (Fig. 2-28). This involves six independent controls; thus, if the body

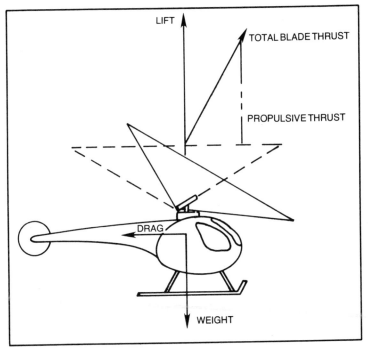

Fig. 2-24. Propulsive thrust.

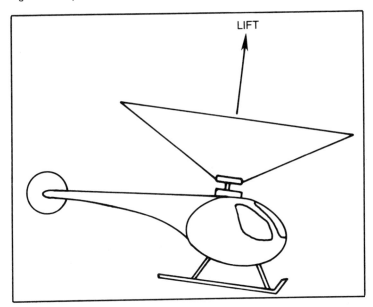

Fig. 2-25. Forward flight.

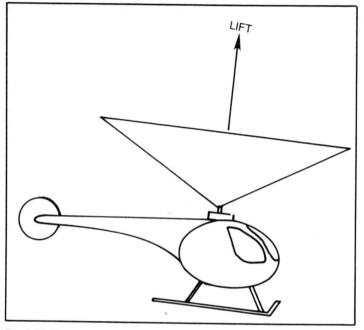

Fig. 2-26. Hovering.

drifts to the side, a force may be exerted to right it again. It would be exceedingly difficult for a man to coordinate the controls of any machine having six independent control systems. Fortunately, it has been possible to reduce this number by coupling together independent controls. Such couplings involve some sacrifice of complete freedom of control of position and attitude in space, but this sacrifice may actually be desirable. The pilot of the helicopter does demand the ability to produce movements about all axes in order to right himself, as when disturbed by a wind gust. He does not demand that he be able to produce movements without producing an accompanying force—in this case, in the longitudinal direction. He therefore sacrifices the ability to maintain force equilibrium, as in hovering, and to rotate his fuselage in pitch at will, so as to attain a desired attitude. By this coupling of pitching moments with longitudinal forces, the necessity for one of the six independent controls is eliminated. The helicopter is thus considered a five-control aircraft, the throttle on the collective pitch being the fifth control. These controls are the *fore and aft cyclic, later cyclic, antitorque* (controlled by the feed), *collective pitch*, and *throttle* (Figs. 2-29 and 2-30).

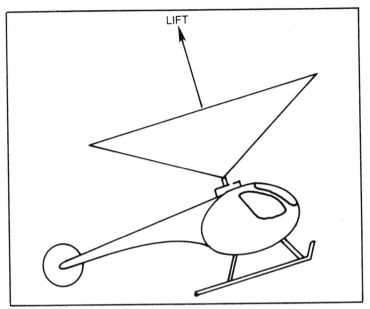

LIFT

Fig. 2-27. Backward flight.

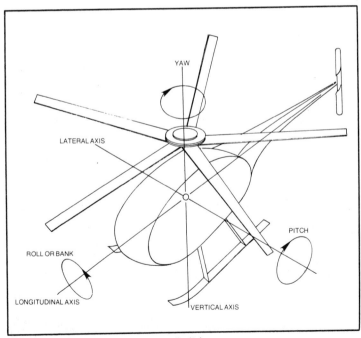

YAW

LATERAL AXIS

PITCH

ROLL OR BANK

LONGITUDINAL AXIS

VERTICAL AXIS

Fig. 2-28. Three axes of flight—yaw, roll, pitch.

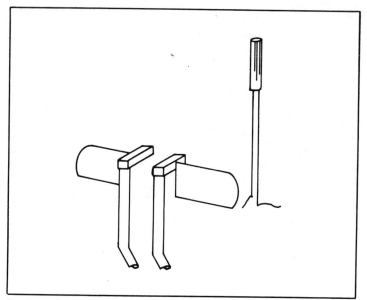

Fig. 2-29. Cyclic control stick.

To successfully accomplish helicopter flight, a pilot must be able to coordinate all the controls. Operation of the helicopter without proper coordination of the controls can result in severe damage to the machine. The flight controls normally employed in present-day helicopters are the cyclic, or azimuth control stick in the pilot's right hand; collective pitch stick, with the motorcycle-type throttle in the pilot's left hand; and foot pedals. Let's take each control separately, then see how each works in coordination with the others.

Collective Pitch System. The collective pitch system, as shown in Fig. 2-31 consists of a collective pitch stick linked to the main rotor blade pitch change arms, a collective balance mechanism, and a collective pitch fraction knob. The collective pitch system controls ascent and descent of the helicopter by varying the pitch of all main rotor blades equally and simultaneously by vertical movement of the swashplate assembly.

The collective pitch control stick is a lever with up-and-down travel located to the pilot's left, and manipulated naturally by the left hand. By raising or lowering the collective pitch stick, you can change the *collective pitch*, the pitch on all of the main rotor blades. Raising the stick increases the pitch; lowering it decreases pitch. If the rotor rpm remains constant, increasing or decreasing the blade pitch causes the helicopter to climb or descend. The throttle, located on the end of the collective pitch control stick, is coordinated with collective pitch to maintain a constant operating rpm. Although most helicopters have a certain amount of designed synchronization between collective pitch and throttle control, the pilot is primarily responsible for throttle control. The motorcycle grip is rolled outward to increase the throttle setting, and rolled inward to decrease it. The collective pitch stick also controls power output by demand. Manifold pressure or torque indicates the output of engine power. As collective pitch is increased, the engine is required to develop more power in order to maintain a constant rpm. To hold a constant power setting, coordination of pitch and throttle correction should be simultaneous. These controls are very sensitive, and correction should be small and smoothly performed to prevent overcontrolling of a reciprocating engine. A turbine engine has more stable speed-controlling mechanisms (Fig. 2-32).

Fuselage Heading. The foot pedals control fuselage heading by changing the pitch on the tail rotor blades. The primary purpose of tail rotor, as explained previously, is to compensate for torque, but fuselage heading is maintained by increasing or decreasing the horizontal thrust of the tail rotor. Applying left rudder causes the nose of the helicopter to turn left. Applying right rudder causes the nose to swing to the right, as shown in Fig. 2-33. It is normal for the single main rotor to turn from right to left as viewed from the pilot's position, and torque would turn the nose of the

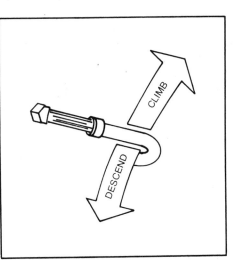

Fig. 2-30. Collective pitch stick and throttle.

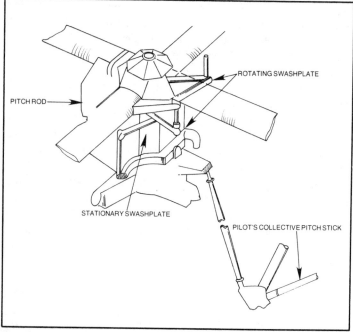

Fig. 2-31. Collective pitch system.

fuselage to the right. The application of left pedal increases the pitch on the tail rotor, which increases horizontal thrust, thus establishing fuselage heading. When the pilot wishes to maintain a constant heading, he keeps just enough pitch on the tail rotor to neutralize the torque effect.

Cyclic Control System The cyclic control system controls the forward, backward, and sideward movement of the helicopter by tilting the main rotor disc in the desired direction of travel. This action is accomplished by varying the pitch of the rotor blades as they rotate. As the pitch of the rotor blades is varied, lift generated by the blades causes the main rotor disc to tilt. The usual mechanical arrangement incorporated to tilt a rotor disc consists of a cyclic stick connected by linkage to a control plate referred to as the *swashplate*. This swashplate is, in turn, connected to the main rotor blades. Cyclic control stick movements are transmitted to the swashplate, which in turn varies the pitch of the rotor blades by means of rods connecting the swashplate and rotating blades.

Figures 2-34 and 2-35 show a closeup view of the swashplate mechanism. The swashplate is mounted coaxially on the rotor mast in such a manner that it can be tilted relative to the rotor shaft, thus

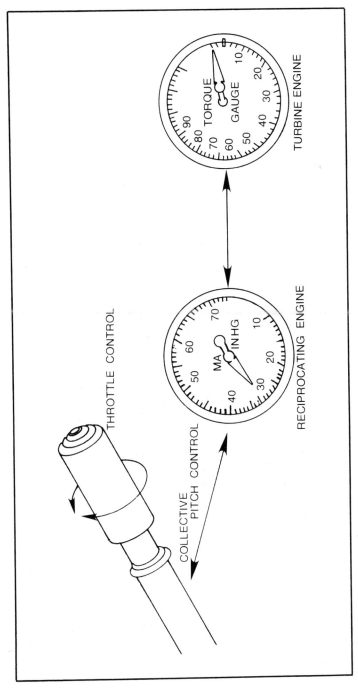

THROTTLE CONTROL

COLLECTIVE
PITCH CONTROL

RECIPROCATING ENGINE

MA
IN HG

TURBINE ENGINE

TORQUE
GAUGE

Fig. 2-32. Throttle control and gauges.

47

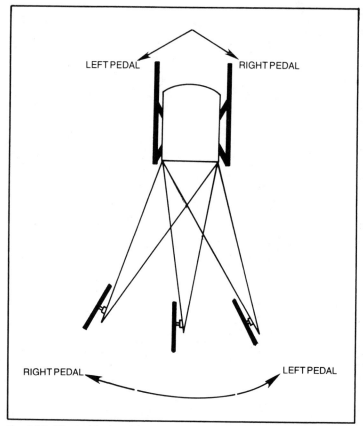

Fig. 2-33. Effect of foot pedals.

acting as a cam to give a reciprocating motion of the pitch control arms. When the swashplate is level, pitch on the main rotor blades will be equal throughout the cycle of rotation, but if the swashplate is tilted, the pitch of the main rotor blades will vary throughout the cycle proportionate to the tilt of the swashplate.

The cyclic control stick, in appearance, is similar to the control stick of a conventional aircraft, and control movement is much the same. Movement of the cycle control stick in any direction causes the main rotor disc to tilt in the same direction. With the cyclic stick in a neutral position, pitch on the main rotor blades will be equal throughout the cycle of rotation, as in hovering or vertical ascent. Forward stick will cause the rotor disc to tilt forward because of gyroscopic precession, to be explained later. As previously stated, resultant thrust is always perpendicular to the tip path plane. When the tip path plane is tilted forward, resultant thrust is inclined forward and propulsive thrust is developed in the direction of tip path plane tilt. The rotor system will move rapidly in the direction of thrust and pull the fuselage in the direction of movement. The fuselage will pitch about the lateral axis and will assume a nose-low attitude. As the cyclic stick is moved in any direction—whether forward, rearward, or sideward—an inclination of the tip path plane will be established in the direction of the cyclic stick movement. The directional speed of the helicopter is controlled by the degree of tilt (Figs. 2-36 and 2-37).

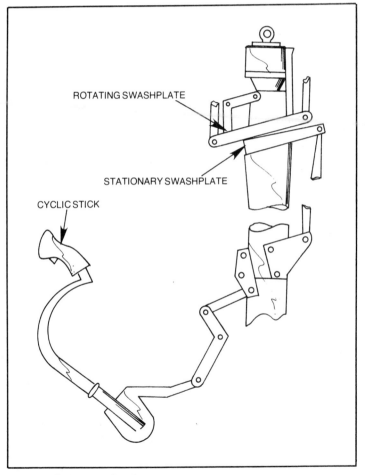

Fig. 2-34. Cyclic control system.

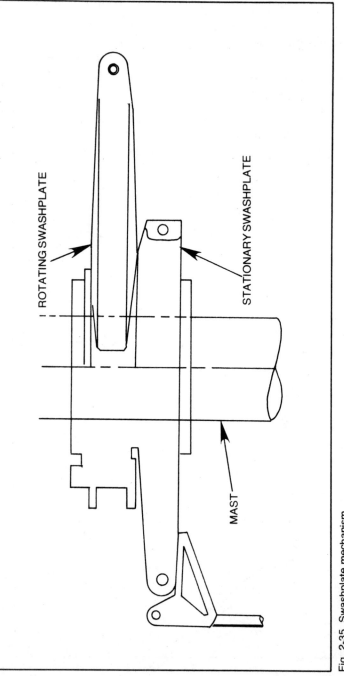

ROTATING SWASHPLATE

STATIONARY SWASHPLATE

MAST

Fig. 2-35. Swashplate mechanism.

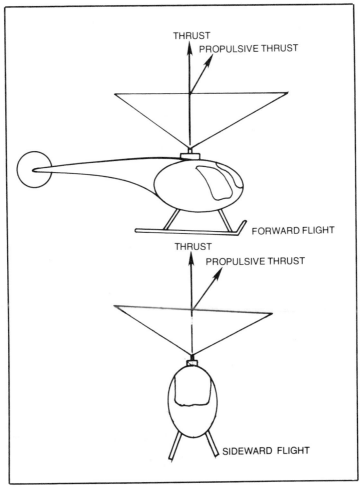

Fig. 2-36. Flight attitudes and propulsive thrust, forward and sideward.

Center of Gravity

The normal center of gravity (CG) location in single-rotor helicopters is shown in Figs. 2-38 and 2-39. All thrust is applied to the fuselage at a single point: the rotor mast. The fuselage, as we have noted before, is somewhat free to swing from this point, much in the fashion of a pendulum. The permissible center of gravity travel is very limited in many helicopters. Some helicopters have only a 4-inch maximum travel. The weight of a pilot, fuel, passengers, cargo, and so on, must be carefully distributed to prevent the helicopter from flying with a dangerous nose-low or nose-high

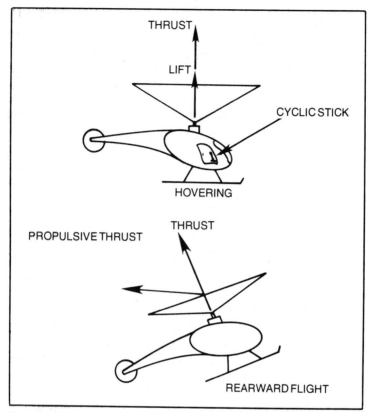

Fig. 2-37. Flight attitudes and propulsive thrust, hover and rearward.

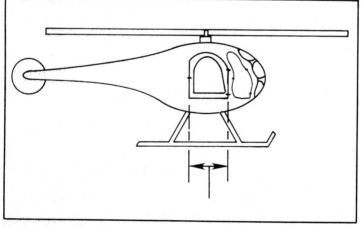

Fig. 2-38. Center of gravity range.

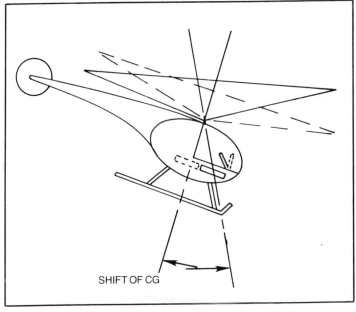

Fig. 2-39. Effect of load on CG shift.

attitude. In newer helicopter designs, efforts have been made to locate the loading compartment directly under the drive shaft to minimize CG travel. For the same reason, the fuel supply may be located at or near the balance point, which is normally on the main drive shaft.

If a helicopter is improperly loaded, not only does the fuselage tilt off the horizontal but the rotor mast, which is attached to the fuselage, tilts the entire rotor system. The cyclic stick controls the amount and the direction of tilt of the rotor system, but the travel on the cyclic control stick is limited. The amount of back stick the pilot can apply to the cyclic control to level the rotor system is limited by the manner in which the helicopter is rigged. If the nose-low attitude assumed by the fuselage, owing to a faulty loading, is in excess of or near the rearward travel limit of the cyclic stick, the pilot may not be able to stop the forward flight of the helicopter. In some helicopters where the fuel cell is located aft, the burning off of fuel will increase the forward CG travel. If the helicopter at takeoff is balanced at its forward CG limit, the pilot may find that, when he pulls the cyclic control back as far as it will go, the helicopter's attitude remains nose low and the rotor system still tilts forward. The pilot cannot slow the helicopter, nor can he raise the nose to land. Needless to say, he then finds himself in a dangerous predicament. The pilot must balance his load laterally, forward, and rearward, so as to remain within CG travel limits. He should be well informed as to the CG travel limits of his particular helicopter and should exercise great care in taking on loads.

Helicopter Rigging

All helicopters require a definite relationship between control position and blade angle for safe flight. This relationship is established by basic rigging. Basic rigging is established by installing control rigging fixtures to locate the control point and a relationship at the swashplate and blade angle. Any variations are corrected by control rod adjustment. By the nature that all helicopters are individuals, each one must be "tuned" by operation and adjustment as required. Because of the minor variations in the blades, the first step after basic rigging is blade tracking. When the blades are sharing the load and the helicopter is flying smoothly, this step is completed. The final step in tuning is establishing the autorotation rpm required for the weight and density altitude as specified in the maintenance manual (Fig. 2-40).

Autorotation

Autorotation is the process of producing lift with airfoils which rotate freely as the air passes up from the bottom, up through the rotor system. Under "power off" conditions, the helicopter will descend; thus, the airflow will be established from the bottom upward, through the rotor system. The rotor is automatically disengaged from the engine by an overrunning clutch, and the necessary power required to overcome parasitic and induced drag of the rotor blades is obtained from the potential energy, due to the helicopter's weight and height above the ground. This potential energy is converted into kinetic energy which is used to rotate the overhead rotor system during descent. In other words, autorotation is a flight condition in which the lifting rotor is driven entirely by action of the air when the rotorcraft is in motion. A helicopter uses autorotation for emergency landings in case of engine failure. During autorotation, the rotor blades turn in the same direction as when engine-driven, but the air passes upward through this rotor system (Fig. 2-41).

While in autorotation, it is essential that the pitch of the rotor blades be reduced materially to minimize drag, thus permitting a high rotor rpm to build up. When the pitch angle of the main rotor

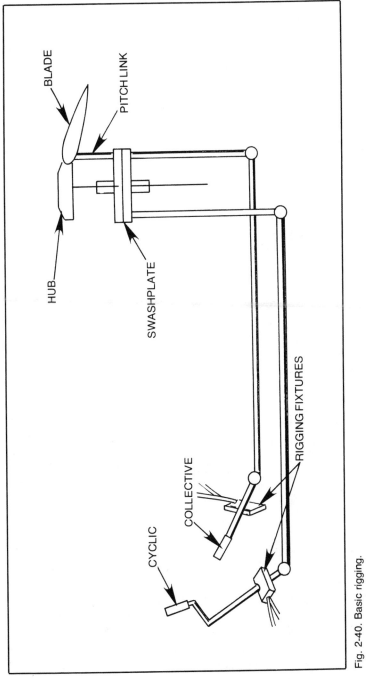

Fig. 2-40. Basic rigging.

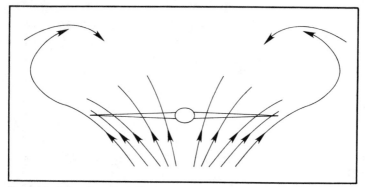

Fig. 2-41. Airflow in autorotation.

blades is low, as shown in the Fig. 2-41, the resultant airfoil lift force lies ahead of the axis of rotation, tending to keep the blade turning in its normal direction of rotation.

Figure 2-42 shows a condition in which the blade pitch angle is too high for satisfactory autorotation. Note that drag is increased and the resultant lift force lies behind the axis of rotation, slowing the rotor. The pilot must reduce the pitch in order to keep the rotor blades turning at sufficient speed.

Gyroscopic Precession

Gyroscopic precession is a characteristic of all rotating bodies. It is the phenomenon by which application of a force perpendicular to the plane of rotation will produce a maximum displacement of the plane approximately 90 degrees later in the direction of rotation. Thus, if a downward force is applied to the side of a rotating disc, (Fig. 2-43) gyroscopic precession will cause the disc plane to tilt approximately 90 degrees later in the direction of rotation, as shown in Fig. 2-44.

The main rotor system of the helicopter displays the phenomenon of gyroscopic precession effectively. The applied force is introduced by pitch change on the main rotor system. Maximum resulting displacement occurs approximately 90 degrees further in the direction of turning, but speed of rotation, weight and diameter of the disc, and friction are factors which determine an actual displacement in a specific system.

Centrifugal Force

Lift, as we know, is derived from the circular motion of the rotor blades. Another major force acting on the blade is *centrifugal*

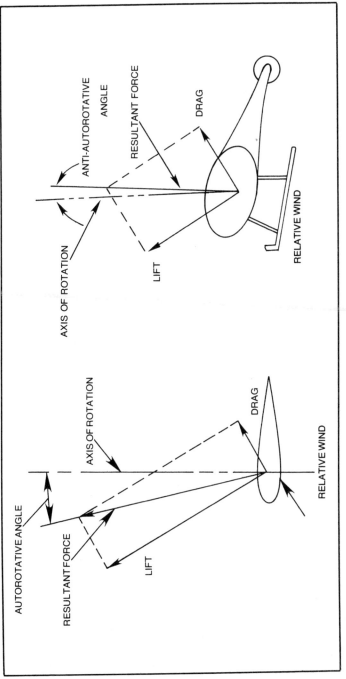

Fig. 2-42. Aerodynamicas of autorotation.

57

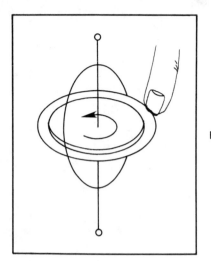

Fig. 2-43. Gyroscopic precession.

force, which acts on all rotating bodies perpendicular to their path and away from the center of rotation. In a helicopter, the rotating rotor system tends to pull the blades away from the rotor head, causing them to form a flat disc area. Centrifugal force at the root of a typical small rotor blade is about 20,000 pounds. The rotor blades depend upon centrifugal force for their rigidity (Fig. 2-45).

Coning Angle and Loading

The rotor blades tend to deflect upward when required to lift or support the weight of the helicopter. This results from the combination of centrifugal force and lift, and is known as *coning* or

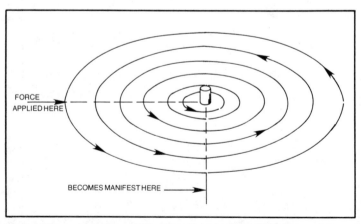

FORCE APPLIED HERE

BECOMES MANIFEST HERE

Fig. 2-44. Force applied to a rotating disc will cause disc to tilt 90 degrees later.

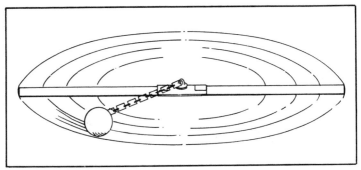

Fig. 2-45. Centrifugal force.

coning angle. The upward deflection of the rotating blades gives the appearance of a cone shape, as depicted in Fig. 2-46. In a fully articulated system, the flapping hinge will provide for the majority of coning action. From this illustration, we can see that as lift forces the blades to support the load of the helicopter, they are deflected upward and form a rotation disc which, when viewed from the side, is in the form of a cone. The coning angle is measured from a plane perpendicular to the shaft to the lowest portion of the cone made by the blades in rotation. In Fig. 2-46, the helicopter is hovering and is lightly loaded. The coning angle is not as high; as the blades are supporting only a normal load, the high rpm of the rotor blades is producing a great deal of centrifugal force which will keep the coning angle at a relatively small value.

   Let us assume, however, that the helicopter is loaded heavily and it is hovering at full power. As we see in Fig. 2-47 the coning angle has increased, for, while full power is being maintained, the blades are supporting more weight. The weight components have

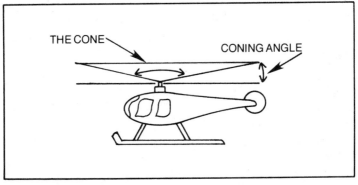

Fig. 2-46. Coning angle.

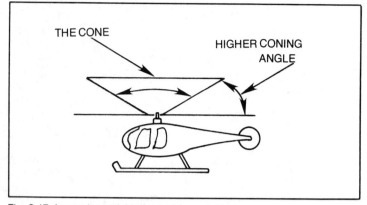

Fig. 2-47. Increasing weight also increases coning angle.

increased in magnitude, while centrifugal force has remained unchanged. The resultant of these two forces, which determines the coning angle, is thus increased and has slightly changed direction upward, increasing coning angle. Now the same situation holds true when rotor speed is decreased, for, with a decrease in rotor speed, there is less centrifugal force, which once again changes the direction and the magnitude of the resultant of the weight and centrifugal force components. Gross weight of the helicopter, in combination with rotor rpm, will determine the degree of coning.

Ground Cushion

Different types of airflow conditions exist on the main rotor. Rotor flow states are the general terms used to describe a certain type of flow condition. A general rotor flow state, where the air is down through the rotor as shown in Fig. 2-48, is known as the normal working state. This flow state occurs during hovering, forward flight, and most powered flight conditions.

As stated previously, during hovering the airflow state is known as the normal working state. When a helicopter is hovering close to the ground, the high pressure region between the helicopter and the ground is called *ground cushion* or *ground effect*, and it aids in supporting the helicopter. Ground cushion or ground effect is a volume of packed air built up between the rotor blades and the ground. The downward flow of air strikes the ground and is partially trapped under the main rotor system. The air packs because it cannot escape as rapidly as the downward flow; therefore, a cushion of slightly compressed air is established. The packed air is denser, thus increasing both the efficiency of the engine and the rotor system (Fig. 2-49). The ground cushion is effective to the height of approximately one-half the rotor diameter. Above this height, the air cannot be effectively trapped; also, the ground cushioning effect is lost at airspeeds in excess of 10 mph. When moving from a hover to forward flight, it is noted in Fig. 2-49 that the blade tips will move into the upward air circulation. This will cause a momentary vibration because of high blade tip loading during the transition from hover to forward flight.

Translational Lift

When hovering four to six feet above the ground in a windless condition, the helicopter is aided by the ground cushion effect. A pilot preparing to move into forward flight will tilt the tip path plane forward. As speed is attained, the helicopter will settle toward the ground for two reasons: first, as the helicopter enters forward flight, it slides off the ground cushion effect, losing the support of the denser air; second, the main rotor system will no longer be devoted completely to lift, but will be divided between lift and thrust. However, when a forward speed of approximately 15 mph is reached, the additional lift developed in horizontal flight, which is known as *translational lift*, becomes effective. The rotor system produces more lift in forward flight because the higher inflow velocity supplies the rotor disc with a greater mass of undisturbed air per unit time upon which to work than it would receive while hovering. Translational efficiency increases with translational speed. This increase in efficiency is cancelled out at some forward speed, usually between 40 and 60 mph forward speed (Fig. 2-50).

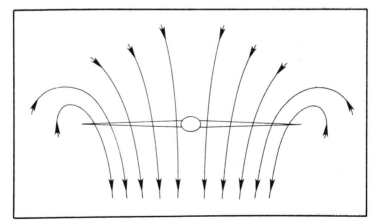

Fig. 2-48. Normal working state of rotor.

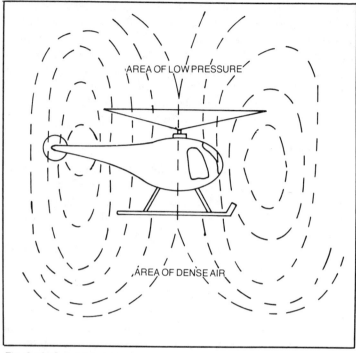

Fig. 2-49. Ground cushion.

Advancing Blade

A helicopter, when in forward flight, has blades moving into the relative wind on one side of the disc area, and moving with the relative wind on the other side of the disc area. As shown in Figs. 2-51 and 2-52, with the helicopter moving to the right, one blade is advancing to the right, in the direction of the flight of the helicopter; hence, *into* the relative wind and, thus, known as the *advancing blade*. The other blade moving in the direction opposite to that of the flight of the helicopter is moving *with* the relative wind on the opposite side of the disc area, and is known as the *retreating* blade. In forward flight, the advancing blade always has the least pitch angle or angle of attack while the retreating blade always has the greatest pitch angle or angle of attack. The speed of the relative wind over an airfoil determines the amount of lift. When hovering in still air, the lift distribution over the rotor disc is uniform. The rotor disc is operating at a constant angular velocity with equal angles of attack; hence, equal lift. In forward flight due to the advancing blade moving into the relative wind on one side of the

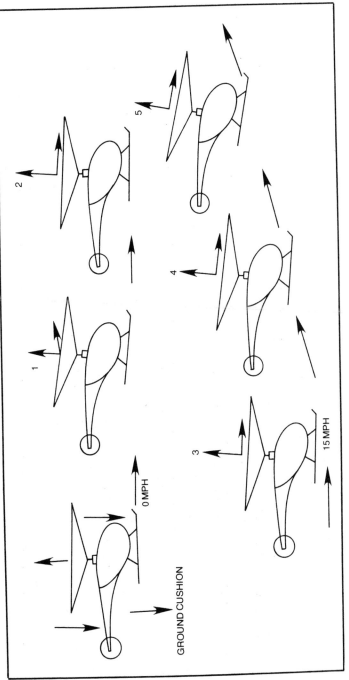

Fig. 2-50. Effective translation lift.

63

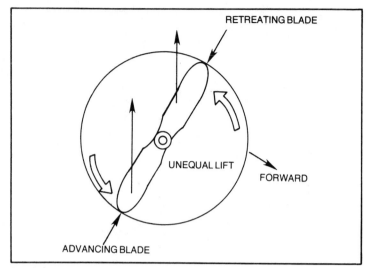

Fig. 2-51. Unequal lift is developed by advancing and retreating blades.

disc area, and retreating blade moving with the relative wind on the other side, we have a condition of unequal lift across the rotor disc, known as *dissymmetry of lift.*

Dissymmetry of lift is created by the horizontal movement of the helicopter at forward flight; the advancing blade, as shown in Fig. 2-53 has rotational speed plus the forward speed plus the forward speed of the helicopter, while the retreating blade, as shown in Fig. 2-53, loses speed in proportion to the forward speed of the helicopter, or has rotational speed minus the speed of the helicopter.

As shown in Fig. 2-54, the most effective lift area in forward flight is at the blade tips, with the least effective lift area being at the center of the disc. As stated previously, upon entering forward flight, the speed of the advancing blade increases equally with the forward speed of the helicopter. At the same time, the speed of the retreating blade decreases proportionally. If our blade tip speed is 300 mph in a zero wind hover and we enter forward flight at a speed of 100 mph, our advancing blade tip speed will increase equally with the forward speed giving up a tip blade speed of 400 mph on the advancing blade, as shown in Fig. 2-55. The retreating blade, as shown on the left, will lose 100 mph, having a tip blade speed of 200 mph. Unless this dissymmetry of lift is compensated for by a change in the coefficient of lift, the helicopter will pitch up and roll over.

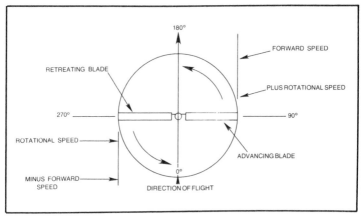

Fig. 2-52. Advancing and retreating blades.

It was this pitching and rolling effect that led many helicopter and autogyro builders to abandon their projects. Juan de la Cierva was the first to realize what caused this rolling effect, and he solved this problem by mounting his autogyro blades individually on flapping hinges. This flapping action automatically corrected the dissymmetry of lift that resulted in forward flight. In Fig. 2-56, the retreating blade flaps downward as the advancing blade flaps upward. During forward flight, the advancing blade will flap higher because it has greater lift, and the retreating blade will flap to a

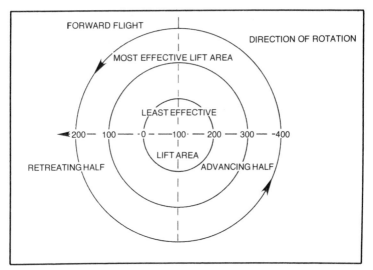

Fig. 2-53. Dissymmetry of lift.

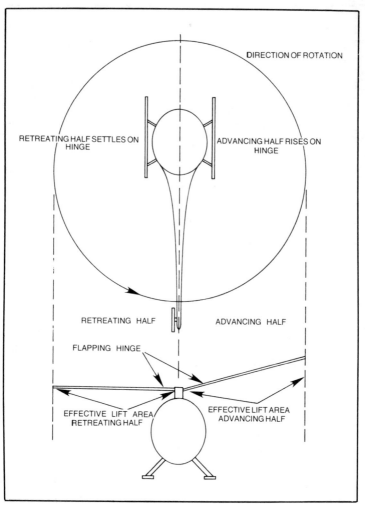

Fig. 2-54. Effective lift areas.

lower angle because it has less lift. As the rotor blade flaps up, the effective lift area is lessened, and, secondly, as the blade flaps upward in the direction of airflow, the angle of attack is reduced. On the retreating path of the disc area, however, reduced airspeed develops less lift; therefore, the retreating blade will have a greater effective lift area and a greater angle of attack, thus increasing overall lift of the low-speed retreating blade; thus, the blades position themselves aerodynamically to equalize lift on the advancing and retreating halves of the disc area.

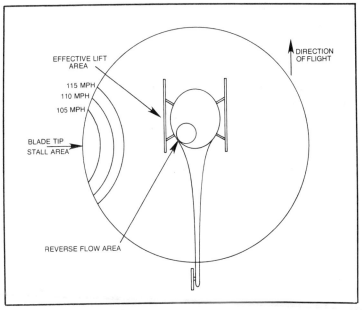

Fig. 2-55. Blade tip speed.

Blade Stall

Whenever the angle of attack on the retreating blade exceeds the stall angle of attack of the blade section, a retreating blade stall results. The stall condition begins at the tip of the retreating blade, since in order to develop the same lift as the advancing blade, the retreating blade must operate at a higher angle of attack due to its lower speed. If the blade pitch is increased or the forward speed increased, the area of the rotor disc becomes larger as the stall area progresses in towards the hub from the tip of the retreating blade.

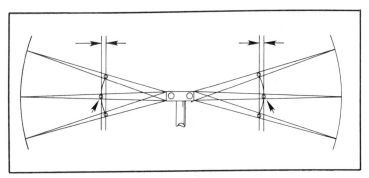

Fig. 2-56. Rotor flapping action corrects dissymmetry of lift.

So, we see that the higher the speed of the helicopter, the greater is the angle of attack of the retreating blade. When the maximum speed of the helicopter is exceeded, the angle of attack of the retreating blade becomes too extreme, causing the retreating blade to stall. Severe blade stall will cause an abrupt pitch-up of the nose of the helicopter because of gyroscopic precession. The advancing blade has relatively uniform low angles of attack and is not subject to the blade stall. A tendency for the retreating blade to stall in forward flight is inherent in all present-day helicopters and is a major factor in limiting their forward speed. Basically, the stall of an airplane wing limits the low-speed possibilities of the fixed-wing aircraft. The stall of a rotor blade limits the high-speed potential of a helicopter. While pilots do disagree to some extent as to the reaction of the aircraft upon entry into blade stall, they generally do agree that a noticeably one-per-rev-per-blade-vibration is the first effect. Actually, the term "one-per-rev-per-blade" implies the number of vibrations per blade per each revolution of the rotor. The vibration takes the frequency of the number of blades in the rotor system as applied to one revolution of the rotor. This vibration is followed by a lifting or pitch-up of the nose and a rolling tendency of the helicopter. When operating at high forward speeds, the conditions most likely to produce blade stall are high blade loading which is caused by low rotor rpm, high density altitude, steep or abrupt turns, and turbulent air. A retreating blade stall does not occur in normal autorotation.

Air Compressibility

It follows that, with a substantially constant rotor rpm, the greater the helicopter forward speed, the greater the advancing blade airspeed. The critical Mach number of the advancing blade now becomes a problem. Compressibility and retreating blade tip stall thus present the ultimate challenge in the performance of the true helicopter. Critical Mach values and drag divergence are not usually a problem; however, they are not to be overlooked. Any helicopter can encounter compressibility when exposed to the right conditions of temperature and altitude. The speed of sound in air at standard sea level conditions is about 760 mph. Since this speed varies with temperature and density, it decreases with increasing altitude, up to about 35,000 feet above this altitude, for several thousand feet, the speed of sound, like that of temperature, does not change much. When the rotor blade airflow is at slower speeds, the air begins to flow into a pattern to receive it, long before the blade itself arrives. It is as if the blade continuously "telegraphed" a warning to the air ahead that it is coming. This telegraphed message moves at the speed of sound. When the blade flies faster than sound, the telegraphed message does not have time to arrive, and the air is unprepared to receive the blade. A wave of compressed air forms ahead of the blade, or is attached to the landing edge. This is called a *shock wave* and results in additional drag. Some separation of the flow may occur behind the shock wave, and may cause an increase in drag and decrease in lift. The transonic flow is less stable than either subsonic or supersonic flow, and causes some blade stability and control problems. The helicopter V_{ne} (never exceed speed) placards limitations are derived considering retreating blade stall and compressibility.

Coriolis Force

In a rotating mechanical system, a force is generated as a result of the system attempting to follow the law of conservation of momentum which states that the total momentum in a closed system is constant. As the blades flap up or down, the center of gravity of the blades moves towards or away from the center of rotation of the blades. This results in a change in the distribution of the mass with respect to the axis of rotation. Since, in both cases the angular moment must be equal, this equality is maintained by the blades speeding up or slowing down an amount which will result in the same angular momentum. This force tending to speed up or to slow down the rotor blade in the plane of rotation is called the *coriolis force*; allowing the blades to hinge at the hub relieves some of this force. This force causes the speed in which the ice skater is spinning to increase when he brings his arms in close to his body, thereby effectively reducing his mass moment of inertia and necessitating an increase in spinning speed to keep the same angular momentum.

Lead/Lag Hinge

The speeding up, slowing down, and horizontal movement of the blade about a vertical hinge is referred to as *hunting*. Lead and lag are the terms used to describe the hunting motion of the rotor blades of a fully articulated system around their lead/lag hinge. At only one time during the flight of the helicopter does the blade operate close to the pure radial position or straight out through the offset hinges, and that is during autorotation. At all other times during operation, the blade is either leading or lagging the mean lag position. During the stopping procedure, as the rotor slows down, the blade, due to its own inertia, will resist slowing down and will lead the pure radial position by a minor amount of the fully articulated system. In starting, the blade will lag far behind the pure radial position until centrifugal force brings it up to its normal operating position. In normal operation, the blade will lag behind the pure radial position due to the drag of the rotor blade. The range experienced during normal operation is caused by the increase or decrease of rotor speed and power. At low power and high rotor speed, the blades will lag less than with low rotor speed and high power. The hunting motion is caused by the flapping of the bladed and drag variations (Fig. 2-57).

Blade Feathering

Although blade flapping during rotation helps to equalize blade lift, it is necessary to make changes in the blade angle of attack about the spanwise axis of the blade as it progresses around the azimuth. This periodic increasing and decreasing of the pitch of the rotor blade by oscillating the blade about its span axis and within the pitch bearing housing is called *feathering*. Feathering motion provides a means for tilting the rotor plane fore, aft, and laterally. Whenever the vertical axis of rotation and the mast do not coincide, cyclic feathering aids the flapping motion in balancing air loads. The shaft axis and the vertical axis of the rotor no longer fall upon the same line. The foward blade is flapping down and the rearward blade is flapping up. Notice in Fig. 2-58 that the mass of the upflapping blade has moved in toward the axis of rotation. Whenever the shaft axis and the vertical axis of the rotor are not the same (when cyclic pitch is being applied), the radius of the blade mass will not be constant and it will have a periodic velocity toward or away from the center of rotation.

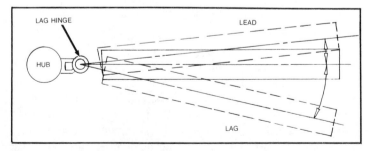

Fig. 2-57. Blade hunting.

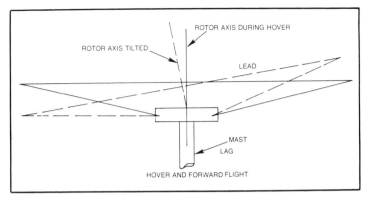

Fig. 2-58. Blade feathering.

Any rotating mass which also has a velocity toward the center of rotation generates a coriolis force in the direction of rotation. When the velocity is away from the center of rotation, the coriolis force is opposite rotation. The first is an accelerating force, the second a decelerating force. The total force on the blade is the sum of the forces on the individual elements. In the cyclicly tilted rotor, coriolis forces cause the blades to hunt forward or backward (lead and lag) (accelerate or decelerate) just enough so that the forces stay in balance and angular momentum is conserved. The coriolis force is minimized by tilting the mast a few degrees forward (Figs. 2-59 and 2-60).

Torque

Torque created by the engine is another force acting on the rotor blades. This phenomenon is relatively easy to understand if a fundamental law of physics is applied. As expressed in Newton's

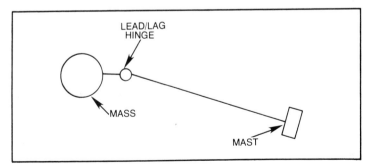

Fig. 2-59. Coriolis force: normal lag position of blade.

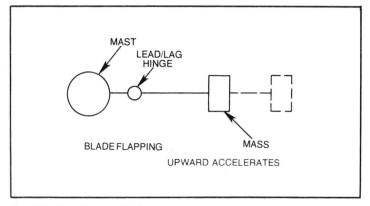

Fig. 2-60. Coriolis force: blade flapping upward accelerates.

third law of motion, "for every action there must be an equal and opposite reaction." When the blades of a helicopter are rotated in one direction by engine power, the torque reaction set up tends to rotate the helicopter fuselage in the opposite direction. Torque produces a movement about the vertical hinge in starting, stopping, acceleration, and certain other conditions of flight.

Here, torque is depicted in Fig. 2-61. The rotation of the engine-driven rotor, turning counterclockwise, causes the clockwise rotation of the fuselage. Torque is of real concern to both pilot and the designer. Adequate means must be provided, not only to counteract torque, but also for positive control for its effect during flight. In the single main rotor helicopter, torque is usually counteracted by a vertically mounted tail rotor which is located on the outboard end of the tail boom (Fig. 2-62). The tail rotor develops horizontal thrust that opposes the torque reaction, and the pilot can vary the amount of horizontal thrust by activating foot pedals which are linked by cables or rods to a pitch-changing mechanism in the tail rotor system.

The helicopter has a tendency to move in the direction of tail rotor thrust; that is, to the right when hovering (Fig. 2-63). This drifting tendency is overcome by the tip path plane of the main rotor tilted slightly to the left. This results in the thrust force action to the left equaled to and compensating the tendency to drift to the right. With high gross weight helicopters, the high torque and required compensation causes the left gear to be considerably lower in a hover and when landing. This lower gear condition can be undesirable; consequently, some designers have the main rotor mast tilted a few degrees to the left.

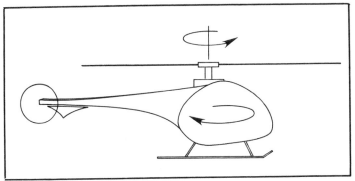

Fig. 2-61. Torque wants to rotate the helicopter opposite the rotor.

Power Settling

At high altitudes, high gross weights, or when operating with reduced power, it may not be possible to maintain level flight due to a lack of power. The phenomenon known as *power settling* is not too important except at certain combinations of rate of descent and

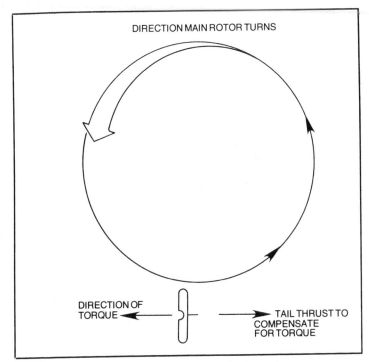

Fig. 2-62. The tail rotor is used to compensate for torque.

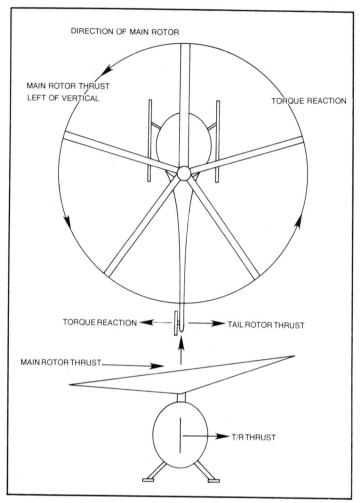

DIRECTION OF MAIN ROTOR

MAIN ROTOR THRUST
LEFT OF VERTICAL

TORQUE REACTION

TORQUE REACTION ← TAIL ROTOR THRUST →

MAIN ROTOR THRUST →

T/R THRUST →

Fig. 2-63. The helicopter will tend to move in the direction of the tail rotor thrust.

low airspeed. When operating at these combinations, power settling becomes critical. Aerodynamic analysis of power settling shows that when a critical power settling condition occurs, roughness and a degeneration of control effectiveness results. As we have seen from previous discussions, rotor downwash approaches maximum values when the helicopter is at or entering the hover. Under certain power and rate of descent combinations, a vortex ring flow state occurs through the rotor. A gigantic recirculation of air takes place in and around the rotor (Fig. 2-64).

The helicopter settles into the air mass that its rotor has just had placed in its attempts to produce adequate lift. The blades attempt to maintain efficiency, but fall short of the desired effect because they are working in their own turbulence. In extreme power settling, the velocity of the recirculating mass becomes so high that full collective pitch and power will not produce sufficient thrust to slow down or control the rate of descent which can exceed 3000 feet per minute. Recovery from this condition is achieved by increasing forward speed (airspeed), decreasing collective pitch, or entering autorotation if altitude and other conditions permit. It can be seen from the above description that considerable loss of altitude may be experienced before power settling is recognized and recovery effected. Because of this fact, conditions tending to cause power settling should be avoided at low altitudes above ground level.

Ground Resonance

The addition of drag hinges substantially relieved the in-plane bending moments caused by periodic air loads and mass forces, but in giving the blade freedom of movement in the plane of rotation, the door was left open to another problem, namely, *ground resonance*. Of the two types of vibrations found in helicopters, ordinary and self-excited, ground resonance is the self-excited type. Self-excited vibrations need no periodic external forces to start or maintain them. When a coupling or interaction occurs between the movement of the rotor blades about their drag hinges and a fore-and-aft or sideward movement of the main rotor shaft

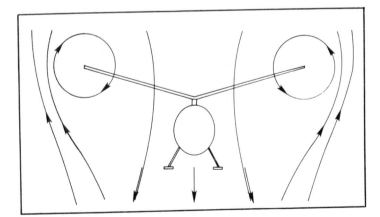

Fig. 2-64. Power settling.

(i.e., the whole aircraft), the result is a self-excited vibration. During resonance, the helicopter rocks fore and aft or sideways with increasing magnitude, with the rotor blades weaving back and forth in the plane of rotation and out of pattern. The phenomenon is known as ground resonance because the vibration occurs when the aircraft is on the ground supported by its relatively soft landing gear, a support conducive to a low frequency movement of the aircraft either fore and aft or sideways. This instability, created by the interaction of a helicopter's rocking on its landing gear and the oscillation of the blades about the drag hinges, can cause destruction to the aircraft. During ground resonance, the blades are definitely out of pattern. If one blade leads while an adjacent blade lags, the resultant out-of-balance condition of the rotor causes the shaft axis to follow the heavy or more centrifugally loaded section of the rotor. Because both the rocking and the movement of the blades in and out of pattern excite each other to greater magnitudes, ground resonance forms an excellent example of negative stability or negative damping. To reiterate, two conditions must exist to cause ground resonance. First, there must be some abnormal lead/lag condition which dynamically unbalances the rotor. This could be caused by a blade badly out of track, a faulty damper, or a peculiar set of landing sequence conditions. Secondly, a reaction between the aircraft and the ground via the landing gear which would aggravate and further unbalance the rotor. When, during the course of a landing, a landing gear reaction occurs that would cause a set of blades already out of pattern to become even further out of phase, and this out-of-phase condition progresses to the point of maximum lead and lag blade displacement, ground resonance will undoubtedly occur. A hard, one-gear landing with a tricycle landing gear would be an example of such a situation. Many pilots will remember instances when a helicopter went into ground resonance when it was in the process of slowly lifting off the ground or was partially airborne. This was particularly true when the helicopter land gear utilized air-oil struts (oleo). The rate of the air spring in the strut varies with its deflection, thus causing the helicopter's natural frequency to vary according to the amount of weight on the gear. A helicopter might be quite stable when all its weight is on the ground, but might experience instability when partially airborne. When resonance is suspected and rotor rpm is within operating range, the immediate application of power and a rapid takeoff will stop this condition. By becoming fully airborne, the helicopter's natural frequency changes. As rolling and lateral natural frequencies attenuate, the interaction of coupling between the blades and the airframe is destroyed and the condition ceases. Adequate system damping and control of the helicopter's natural frequencies have, to all intents and purposes, practically eliminated ground resonance as an operating problem. Engineers accomplished this by refinements resulting from intimate studies of blade dampers, oleo struts, spring rates, tire/spring rates, and landing gear types and treads. It is apparent that drag hinges are mandatory. It is also apparent that the drag hinges permit the movement of the blade in the plane of rotation which, when the aircraft is on the ground, can result in resonance when coupled with other factors. In flight, we desire that the blades have substantial freedom of movement in the plane of rotation. On the ground, we would like to have the blades fixed in the plane of rotation (Fig. 2-65).

Obviously, some sort of compromise is called for; consequently, the main rotor damper is required (Fig. 2-66). In-plane movements of the blade in flight, dictated by varying air loads and/or coriolis forces, are not adversely limited by damper action. A primary utility of the damper lies in its resonance inhibiting abilities. As a matter of interest, ground resonance is the only major self-excited vibration applicable to helicopters utilizing fully articulated rotor systems. Rotor-stimulated vibrations which occur at frequencies that are even multiples of rotor speed, intermittent air forces, and all other types of ordinary vibrations will not be discussed as they are beyond the scope of this work.

Vibration

Of interest to maintenance personnel, however, is the fact that the vibrations can be classified into three basic categories. They are of low, medium, and high frequencies. Low frequency vibrations stem from the unit with the lowest rpm which is, of course, the main rotor. If these vibrations are abnormal, all elements of the blades and rotor head assemblies are suspect. Rotor blades, for example, could be out of track or physically damaged. They could be out of spanwise or pitching moment balance. Many things can cause variations in profile drag (dire, etc.). In the rotor head, it would be well to look for binding of components, excessive play in and between components, improper torques, bad dampers and bad bearings, to mention just a few. Medium frequency vibrations generally stem from the tail rotor assembly. Troubleshooting this vibration calls for roughly the

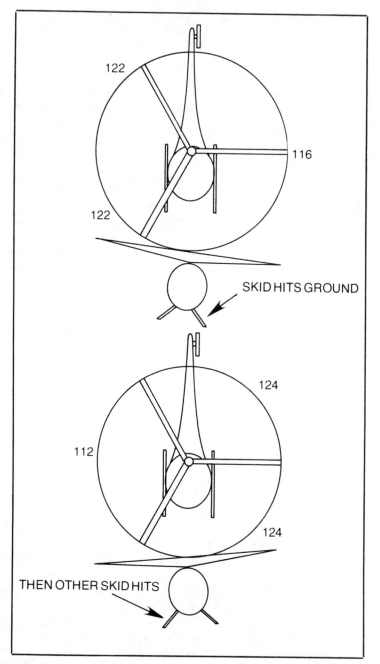

SKID HITS GROUND

THEN OTHER SKID HITS

Fig. 2-65. Ground resonance.

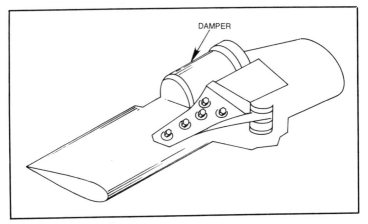

Fig. 2-66. Main rotor damper.

same procedure as used with the main rotor. High frequency vibrations generally originate from the engine and shafting being driven at high rpm. Maintenance handbooks generally give directions for the isolation of vibration troubles.

Chapter 3

Operating the Helicopter's Controls

The information contained in this chapter, along with that imparted in the previous chapters, is intended as a guide to the student and/or fixed-wing pilot wishing to more fully understand the principles of rotary-wing flight and further will describe the skills required of the pilot to actually fly the helicopter. This chapter can be a useful guide to pilots in training as a source of supplemental study. Rotary-wing flight training should include, in this author's opinion, extensive academic study to fully acquaint the student, or fixed-wing transitional pilot, with all of the very complex principles involved in rotary-wing flight. When all of the different modes of rotary-wing flight are considered, it should be clear that we are dealing with very involved and extensive flight possibilities. To utilize all of its capabilities will require much academic as well as hands-on flight training.

It has been said that "flying is flying" and there are many very close similarities between rotary and fixed-wing flight characteristics. However, as we have seen in earlier chapters, there are many variations of these basic principles when applied to helicopters. It is in understanding these differences, along with the study of the special characteristics of rotary-wing flight, that will enable one to develop the necessary proficiency to become a good and safe helicopter pilot.

Weather, navigation, and radio communications, along with adherence to FAA regulations, are a few items that do not change regardless of what type of aircraft you are flying. Instrument interpretation, drift correction, and air judgment that fixed-wing pilots already have learned will prove also to be assets when making the transition to rotary-wing flight. The helicopter, much like its fixed-wing counterpart, is flown by *attitude*, and a knowledge and skill acquired here will prove invaluable in allowing the fixed-wing pilot to make the transition. He can then acquire proficiency faster than the student with no previous flight experience.

It is the unique and varied flight possibilities of the helicopter that demand from the pilot better-than-average coordination and sensitivity to any particular flight condition. The helicopter, as stated many times, can fly forward, backward, sideways, hover, and make both running and almost straight up or down landings and takeoffs. If the would-be helicopter pilot is to become both skillful and safe, he must concentrate on developing such coordination and sensitivity for the controls. This facet of rotary-wing flying cannot be over emphasized, and is probably the single most important aspect of actual flight there is.

Basic Principles

Nowhere is this coordination and sensitivity of the controls more important or better emphasized than in the handling of the pitch and throttle controls. Here, more than any other, must the student practice and practice until his coordination and sensitivity for these two controls become almost instinctive and second nature (Fig. 3-1).

The throttle is located on the end of the collective pitch control stick and controls the rpm of the engine and rotor. The collective pitch stick is used to control the altitude of the craft. In order to fly the helicopter, the pilot must coordinate his throttle and collective pitch to one another. It is through the use of these two controls that the pilot is able to maintain a constant operating rpm. There is built into most helicopters a certain degree of synchronization, but it is primarily in the hands of the pilot to effect the actual control. *If there is one key element to safe and skillful rotary-wing flight, this is it.*

Rpm is controlled by the throttle corrections and changes are made by reference to the tachometers. Collective pitch corrections and changes are made by reference to the manifold pressure gauge. Again, these two functions must be coordinated; therefore, simultaneous checking of both gauges is required during flight. Rpm is controlled by the throttle and manifold pressure by the collective pitch stick (normally referred to as the collective stick). *Anytime you adjust the setting of either the throttle or the collective stick you will affect the other.* That is, if you alter the rpm setting on the throttle, you will normally affect the manifold pressure, and vice versa. When you raise the collective stick you will raise the manifold pressure and cause a decrease in rpm's, which will require an adjustment of the throttle to compensate. It follows then, that when you increase rpm by adjusting the throttles, you cause a decrease in manifold pressure; again, this will require an adjustment of the collective stick to compensate. Because of this relationship, adjustments should be kept as small and smooth as possible. The throttles are especially sensitive to adjustment. To hold a constant power setting it is then necessary to coordinate the adjustment and/or control of both the throttle and collective stick. The following should be commited not only to memory, but should be accomplished almost without being consciously aware of it to the would-be helicopter pilot.

A. When you adjust the throttles to:

1. Increase rpm, you decrease manifold pressure; therefore, decrease collective stick to maintain constant rpm.

2. Decrease rpm, you increase manifold pressure; therefore, decrease collective stick to maintain constant rpm.

B. When you adjust the collective pitch stick to:

1. Increase collective pitch, you increase manifold pressure and decrease rpm; therefore, you must increase throttle.

2. Decrease collective pitch, you decrease manifold pressure and increase rpm; therefore, you must decrease throttle.

This *must* be done in order to maintain a constant power setting. Remember!

An increase in rpm = A decrease in manifold pressure.

A decrease in rpm = An increase in manifold pressure.

An increase in manifold pressure = A decrease in rpm.

A decrease in manifold pressure = An increase in rpm.

TO MAINTAIN A CONSTANT POWER SETTING, ANY CHANGE IN THE THROTTLE MUST BE SIMULTANEOUSLY MADE WITH A CORRESPONDING CHANGE IN COLLECTIVE PITCH. COLLECTIVE PITCH MUST BE SIMULTANEOUSLY MADE WITH A CORRESPONDING CHANGE IN THROTTLE.

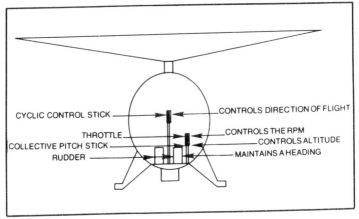

Fig. 3-1. Helicopter controls.

This procedure holds true as long as you are operating at less than full throttle. When operating at a maximum power you are decreasing your safety factor by being unable to correct for any increase in collective pitch. For example, when operating at full power and you make an increase in collective pitch by raising the stick, you will bring about an increase in manifold pressure and, therefore, cause a decrease in rpm. If you are operating at full power you will be unable to compensate for this drop in rpm. You cannot further increase rpm since it is already at maximum. This is the reason that rotary-wing flight should *always* be accomplished with the least throttle and collective pitch that will allow you to complete the flight requirement. To use more is not only wasteful, but can also be dangerous by limiting your ability to control your flight conditions. Safety should be the prime concern of every pilot at all times, and the remaining power capability of your ship is your safety margin in rotary-wing aircraft. To fly without a reasonable safety margin is foolhardly and dangerous not only to the pilot and passengers, but also to persons on the ground who might be in the path of a falling ship. *Safe flying is the only good flying.*

Straight and Level Flight

When flying a rotary-wing aircraft in a straight, level condition, airspeed will be determined primarily by the attitude of the aircraft. The attitude of the aircraft is controlled or adjusted by the use of the cyclic pitch stick (most often referred to as the cyclic stick). Altitude, as previously stated, is maintained and/or controlled by the simultaneous use of the throttle and the collective stick. To recap, speed of the aircraft is maintained by the cyclic stick and altitude by the use of the collective stick. These two controls are important and their function should be known *intimately* to the perspective pilot. Here lies one of the primary differences that exist between fixed and rotary-wing aircraft. While the fixed-wing craft can be flown with the use of one hand at times, the rotary-wing aircraft is *at all times a two hands-on aircraft*. It follows that greater coordination will be required from the rotary-wing aircraft pilot to activate and utilize two separate controls at the same time.

When any change in collective stick is made, while maintaining a constant airspeed, a relative change will take place in the altitude of the craft. If, for example, you increase collective and maintain a constant rpm by the use of the throttle, you will begin to climb or gain altitude. A decrease in collective, with a constant rpm, will bring about a loss of altitude. This is true whenever you are flying in a level manner.

A change in airspeed during straight and level flight may be brought about by the following actions on the collective and cyclic control sticks. An increase in airspeed may be accomplished by increasing the collective to obtain greater power, while tilting the cyclic stick slightly forward. This will change the attitude of the craft, resulting in an increase in airspeed. In order to decrease airspeed, you likewise will decrease collective. To bring about a decrease in power, while tilting the cyclic stick slightly back, changing the attitude of the aircraft; thus, reducing the speed correspondingly.

It should be noted that airspeed and attitude of a rotary-wing aircraft are directly and proportionally related to one another. These are primarily controlled by the cyclic stick. The ship's attitude during straight and level flight is controlled by the cyclic stick, which, in turn, controls the airspeed. Since the helicopter's airspeed is controlled by the cyclic stick, the cyclic stick controls the speed of the aircraft.

Cyclic stick control is like most others on the helicopter: quite sensitive. However, there is a slight delay between cyclic control and reaction of the aircraft. The greatest danger in cyclic control is that of over-control, which is due to this slight delay in reaction time of the ship to the controls. This requires greater care when making cyclic stick changes to avoid the real danger of over-control. There is a natural tendency to hold a correction *too* long; over-correcting for the problem or desired change in attitude. Should, for example, the nose of the ship raise or lower from the level flight attitude, you bring the cyclic stick back slightly or move it forward slightly to correct. Holding this correction too long, such as until the ship's nose has returned to normal level flight attitude, over-correction will have taken place by the time you return the cyclic stick to its normal position, and a further counter-correction will be required. The pilot must develop the instinct through actual flight practice as to when to return the cyclic stick to neutral to effect just the amount of attitude change that is desired and/or required. Due to the delay in reaction time between the cyclic control and the actual movement of the ship, this instinctive anticipation of the continued movement is necessary on the part of the pilot. Fortunately, it is rapidly developed during flight training and need not be a concern for most student pilots, as evidenced by the very high success rate enjoyed by most rotary-wing flight schools throughout the world. It requires only that the pilot remember that once a change in attitude is started by an action on the cyclic stick, it will continue to change for a moment after the cyclic stick is returned to its neutral position. This is a definite characteristic of all cyclic stick control.

Hovering

One of the most fascinating characteristics of the helicopter is its ability to hover. No aspect of the helicopter has intrigued onlookers more than this. Hovering, or the ability to fly virtually motionless over a single spot on the ground, is one of the major advantages that rotary-wing aircraft have over conventional fixed-wing aircraft. This ability to fly motionless over a single spot on the ground, while maintaining a constant heading and altitude, has proven to be one of its most valuable assets.

This particular pattern of flight requires a great deal of skill and coordination on the part of the pilot. During this maneuver the pilot's concentration on the problem of flight must be *completely* fixed on flying the ship and nothing else. In order to hover, the pilot must not only utilize the three major controls of the helicopter, but also must coordinate them with a very high degree of skill. The three controls involved in the maneuver are:

1. The *cyclic stick*, which is used to maintain the ship at zero speed incline.
2. The *collective stick*, which is used to maintain the ship's attitude.
3. The *rudder pedals*, which are used to maintain a constant heading for the ship.

The proper coordination of these three controls is mandatory for a successful execution of this flight pattern and/or maneuver. Failure to properly maintain and one of these controls, and to coordinate it with the other two controls, will result in drift from the desired hovering position. This drift will be in the form of a movement from one or more of the flight pattern positions of the hover. They are:

1. Constant altitude.
2. Constant heading.
3. A zero speed condition in any horizontal direction over the hover spot.

The importance of the coordination of these three controls cannot be overemphasized, as well as the proper utilization of them to maintain the desired hovering effect. Incorrect or improper utilization of any one of these controls will not only cause that particular aspect of the maneuver to fail, but will cause a correction to be required on the others to reestablish the desired condition over the designated location.

The pilot's corrections during this maneuver must be of a smooth pressure type, rather than abrupt movements. Corrections must be *small, smooth,* and *coordinated.* Any abrupt changes on the controls will result in a different movement of the hover position. Over-control is probably the single most common error of the student or inexperienced pilot. Hovering, with any degree of precision, can only be accomplished when the pilot can coordinate both hands and feet while utilizing his eyes and senses to the surrounding conditions.

As in straight and level flight, it is the attitude of the aircraft that determines horizontal movement over the ground. The correct attitude for the craft will vary according to wind conditions and balance to keep it motionless over a single spot. It will be found that there will always be some attitude that will allow the helicopter to hover motionless over a single spot on the ground. This attitude can usually be found only by experimentation, but will come more readily with increased experience. Once the proper attitude has been determined, it can be maintained quite easily by awareness of the ever-changing conditions around you. Corrections can be made before the ship will move off the spot by awareness of the constantly changing factors in the air. By maintaining a constant feel of the cyclic stick, the pilot can utilize just the right amount of pressure to counteract the changing conditions around the ship. Thus, the ship will not drift from its desired position. When hovering in a single rotor-type helicopter, it will be found necessary to maintain a slight pressure on the rudder pedals to prevent the engine torque from causing the ship to rotate in a direction opposite that of the main rotor rotation. If it is desired to alter the heading of the ship while hovering, pressure should be increased on the appropriate rudder pedal until the ship begins a smooth, yet slow turning action about its axis. Should an abrupt movement of the rudder pedals take place, instead of a slight increasing of pressure, the nose of the ship will tend to jerk around in place of the slow, smooth rotation brought about by gradually increasing the pressure on the pedals.

Cyclic stick control, like the rudder pedal control, requires a slow and even pressure approach. Should the helicopter begin to move forwards or backwards, a slight increase in pressure on the cyclic stick will stop this movement. If the ship is beginning to move forward, a slight pressure on the cyclic stick is called for; if the movement is backwards, a slight forward pressure on the cyclic stick is required.

The pilot should be constantly alert to even the slightest movement of the ship and should act at once. Corrections should be made immediately before the movement becomes excessive and unable to be corrected with a single control action. If corrections are not made at the first sign of movement, it will in all likelihood be necessary to make several small correction to stop the action, if over-controlling the ship is to be avoided. If the action has gone too far, it will be found that corrections to *all* controls may be required to return the aircraft to its original position.

As stated earlier, altitude is controlled by use of the collective stick and throttle. During hovering, this throttle, collective stick combination hold the ship at a constant altitude. Just as with cyclic stick control of the ship's attitude for zero speed attitude, varying conditions will require experimentation to determine correct collective pitch to maintain a constant altitude. The elements that affect collective pitch are such things as air density, wind conditions, and gross weight. Collective stick manipulation need not be great except during strong and gusty winds when extensive varying of the collective stick may be required to maintain a constant and unvarying altitude for hovering.

Proper use of the three major control systems are required for a truly precision and constant hovering maneuver. It would be well for the student pilot to become very familiar with these controls, their location, and function. Once again, we must suggest that they need not only be put to memory, but they must be practiced and understood until they become second nature. It cannot be stated too often that a *thorough* understanding of the principles of flight and aerodynamics of the helicopter be studied both academically and put into practice and proven to the student pilot. Nothing can impart knowledge as hands-on experience in proving the theories in practice.

Normal Climbing and Descending

Climbing and descending are considered vertical flight maneuvers just as hovering. The same controls used to maintain the ship from climbing or descending during hover are used normally to climb and descend. Altitude is controlled, as stated before, by use of the collective pitch stick and throttle. To climb or descend, you need only increase collective while maintaining constant rpm; to descend, decrease collective while maintaining constant rpm. Just as in hovering, we are normally concerned with heading and airspeed. These two actions are controlled by the rudder pedals and the cyclic stick, respectively.

Climbing is accomplished by the following technique. Increase collective pitch to obtain the desired or required rate of climb. While achieving this climb rate, control the airspeed by holding the attitude of the ship with the cyclic stick. Simultaneously, apply a small amount of pressure to the rudder pedals to prevent nose yaw due to the increased torque. During the climb maneuver, the helicopter's airspeed may be less than the cruising speed of the ship. If this occurs upon leveling off, do not reduce collective pitch until cruising speed has been reestablished.

Descending is really just the opposite of climbing and is controlled in almost an opposite manner. Decrease collective pitch while controlling the throttle until the desired, or required, rate of descent is obtained. Again, control the airspeed by adjusting the attitude of the craft with the cyclic stick. Since torque is normally reduced during descent, the rudder pedals will again require some pressure to maintain a specific heading.

During either climbing or descending, just as in normal flight, change in power requires a coordination between collective pitch stick, throttle, and the rudders. We should also review some basic aerodynamics of weight and thrust. Whenever a rotary-wing craft is hovering, the main rotor supplies the necessary lift to support the ship's weight. When a rotary-wing craft is climbing in a normal manner, the main rotor must not only support the ship's weight, but also supply the thrust required to bring about a vertical rise of the ship. The power used just for lift, while hovering, must now perform *two* tasks: it must provide power to support the weight of the ship and the power required to move that ship upwards in a vertical direction.

The Standard Takeoff

Normally, a standard takeoff will involve two maneuvers; they are hovering and horizontal climbing flight. The process will require care, coordination, and the pilot's undivided attention. The standard takeoff begins with a vertical ascent, which is nothing more than a hover in which the helicopter is allowed to drift upwards. Then, the aircraft is put into the climbing maneuver, with some forward speed, until the desired altitude and airspeed are achieved. The standard takeoff maneuver, while simple and straightforward, requires some careful thought and consideration to execute properly (Fig. 3-2).

When at all possible, a takeoff should be made into the wind. A sighting point on the ground 20 feet in front of the helicopter should be picked for reference purposes during the maneuver. This reference point is used to assist the pilot in keeping the nose of the helicopter on the proper heading during the first part of the takeoff. The cyclic stick and the rudder pedals should be in their neutral positions, while the collective stick should be in its full low position.

Gradually increase the throttles until takeoff rpm is achieved. Next, increase collective pitch slowly while increasing throttles to maintain rpm. At this point you will need to adjust cyclic stick control to prevent the ship from trying to move away from the spot. The increased collective pitch will cause the helicopter to become airborne. Just prior to becoming airborne, you will have to increase rudder pressure to compensate for engine torque. As power and collective pitch are increased, additional cyclic and rudder adjustments will be required to compensate for increased tendencies to move out of a true vertical ascent, and to compensate for the increasing engine torque.

When the ship becomes airborne, it is merely a matter of allowing a vertical ascent to take place. This is achieved by working the controls, as for hovering, except that additional collective is applied to cause the aircraft to rise vertically out of the hover. During the maneuver, cyclic is maintained to prevent any sideways, forwards, or backwards motion. The rudder pedals must be utilized to maintain the craft's nose on a definite heading. The reference point that was selected on the ground is used for this purpose.

If the helicopter is one utilizing an articulated rotor system, the pilot will have to exercise additional caution since his ship will be subject to ground resonance. The pilot must be sure of his takeoff technique to prevent a dangerous vibration being set up by the ground resonance. A study of the previous chapter on the aerodynamics of helicopter flight will show that ground resonance is the result of poor landing and takeoff techniques in helicopters with articulated main rotor systems.

The vertical ascent should be continued until the aircraft is approximately eight feet into the air. At this point, the pilot should begin the combined climbing and directional flight speed maneuver. The tip plane path of the main rotor system should be tilted slightly in the direction that the pilot wishes to go by moving the cyclic stick in that direction. Collective pitch must be adjusted and coordinated with throttle to maintain rpm to achieve the desired climb rate. During this climb, and forward directional flight maneuver, the cyclic pitch should be increased gradually to develop the desired airspeed. When the desired altitude and airspeed is achieved, collective is lowered until the ship is no longer gaining altitude. The throttles are coordinated to maintain a constant rpm as the ship is now flown in the normal horizontal directional flight manner.

The Standard Landing

The standard landing is in reality a complete reverse of the standard takeoff. Executing this reverse pattern requires some special considerations, controls, and observations. Also, it will be necessary to watch out for some special pitfalls during this particular maneuver. The helicopter should never be allowed to touch down while drifting. There is a *very real* and present danger that a drifting helicopter may tip over. No attempt should be made to have all the landing gear touch down at one time. Such an attempt will usually result in a drifting landing. The cyclic stick should be held in whatever position is required to maintain a driftless landing, disregarding completely which gear it causes to touch down first. One last admonishment, and that is, collective pitch should never be lowered so much, and descent achieved so fast, as to necessitate raising the collective stick to prevent a hard landing. This could prove to be a most dangerous approach (Fig. 3-3).

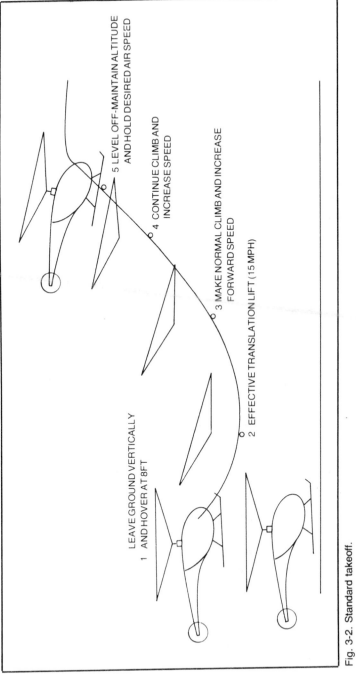

5 LEVEL OFF - MAINTAIN ALTITUDE AND HOLD DESIRED AIR SPEED

4 CONTINUE CLIMB AND INCREASE SPEED

3 MAKE NORMAL CLIMB AND INCREASE FORWARD SPEED

2 EFFECTIVE TRANSLATION LIFT (15 MPH)

1 LEAVE GROUND VERTICALLY AND HOVER AT 8 FT

Fig. 3-2. Standard takeoff.

91

The standard landing begins with what is referred to as the *power glide approach*. From this approach we can learn the basics of power glide control. For those pilots making the transition from fixed to rotary-wing aircraft, we can compare this approach to the power approach of a fixed-wing aircraft. Usually, this is a somewhat shallow approach, but this will depend, however, to a great extent on the type of helicopter being used.

The landing should commence from a standard traffic pattern altitude and into the wind. From here the pilot should begin slowing the helicopter down to the desired groundspeed while maintaining a constant altitude. As a rule, this groundspeed should be somewhere between 40 and 50 mph (indicated). Achieving this groundspeed will necessitate an adjustment to the rudder pedals to compensate for the decreased engine torque and to keep the nose of the ship lined up with the intended landing spot on the ground. The desired groundspeed should be maintained throughout the entire approach. This is accomplished by the use of the cyclic pitch, but will require some coordination with the collective and throttles, as well as some rudder control for the changing power requirements.

Once the appropriate groundspeed and approach are achieved, begin to decrease collective until the required rate of descent is achieved. The required rate of descent is one which, combined with the groundspeed, will bring the helicopter over the landing site at just the right altitude to begin the hovering descent to the ground. This is referred to as the *glide angle*. The glide angle (rate of descent at a given airspeed) is controlled primarily by the collective pitch, the groundspeed by the cyclic pitch, and the heading by the rudder pedals. Any corrections to the collective or the cyclic pitch will most assuredly mandate a correction to the other controls. Corrections for angle of glide, rate of descent and/or groundspeed must be coordinated with the other controls to result in the desired effect.

The most important and critical part of the entire maneuver is the point where you make the transition between approach and hover. This altitude cannot be called out specifically, as it will vary according to all conditions affecting performance and weather. As a guide, 60 to 100 feet may be considered as normal. Once the transition point is reached, the pilot must begin to increase collective in order to bring about a halt to the descent of the helicopter.

As collective is increased, the throttle must be adjusted to maintain a constant rpm. This increase in throttle will call for some

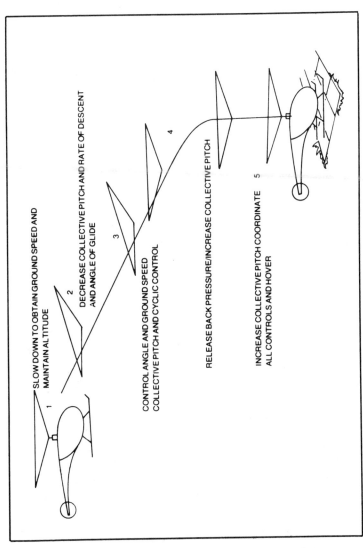

SLOW DOWN TO OBTAIN GROUND SPEED AND
MAINTAIN ALTITUDE

1

2 DECREASE COLLECTIVE PITCH AND RATE OF DESCENT
AND ANGLE OF GLIDE

3

4

CONTROL ANGLE AND GROUND SPEED
COLLECTIVE PITCH AND CYCLIC CONTROL

RELEASE BACK PRESSURE/INCREASE COLLECTIVE PITCH

INCREASE COLLECTIVE PITCH COORDINATE   5
ALL CONTROLS AND HOVER

Fig. 3-3. Standard landing.

rudder correction, due to the increased torque of the engine. This will be in the opposite direction of that needed during the approach. Simultaneously, it becomes necessary to ease back cyclic control pressure so the ship can assume a level attitude. If this were not done, and a tail low attitude were allowed to continue during hover and final descent, the tail rotor might strike the ground. The reason for the cyclic pressure the pilot had been holding was to slow down the ship's forward motion during this approach.

As the helicopter approaches hover, the descent of the ship should be halted completely. There probably should be some slight forward motion to help prevent the student pilot from letting the tail get too low while obtaining a zero groundspeed condition. There is a natural tendency to slightly over-control when slowing the ship to zero groundspeed for hover. This tendency to over-control usually results in the tail being too low and a true level attitude during landing is lost. There is the danger that if it is not corrected before touchdown, the tail may strike the ground, damaging the ship and possibly causing injury to the pilot and passengers.

Again, there are a few conditions and precautions the student pilot should be aware of. There is a tendency for the helicopter to want to balloon slightly as it begins to pick up ground cushion. This can easily be remedied by a small decrease in collective to prevent any gain in altitude. Remember, any change in either collective, throttle, and/or cyclic will necessitate a change in the other controls.

The single most important factor in successful standard landings is a constant apparent groundspeed. This can be accomplished by carefully and consistantly checking apparent groundspeed with reference to the ground. When the pilot has developed the ability to repeatedly attain the same groundspeed in all landings, a constant angle of glide approach will result regardless of other conditions over which the pilot will have little or no control. Careful checking of apparent groundspeed against indicated airspeed will also indicate when a downwind approach is underway. This will be indicated when the airspeed indicator is reading zero and there is still some forward motion taking place. Next, the pilot can estimate the wind in the same way. The higher the initial airspeed that is indicated, once an apparent groundspeed has been established, the greater the wind; and consequently, the lower the indicated airspeed, the lower the wind. Making such use of the airspeed indicator during the standard landing can provide a good deal of useful information. It should be remembered that this is *only* a backup source of information and control during the standard landing and should be based on apparent groundspeed by reference to the ground.

Sideways and Backward Flight

Flying sideways and/or backwards in a helicopter is not difficult, nor is it in any way unusual. It is, in fact, a perfectly normal maneuver in a rotary-wing aircraft. To fly a helicopter in any given horizontal direction, you merely change the attitude or pitch plane path of the aircraft by tilting the cyclic stick in the direction you wish to go. This sounds simple, and after practice with coordinating the controls, it is quite simple. The actual maneuver of changing or setting a direction has been covered elsewhere in this chapter and need not be covered again in detail. However, there are a few precautions and suggestions that can be made in reference to sideways and backwards flight specifically that will be of use.

Before attempting either sideways or backwards flight, a series of turns should be made to ascertain that the area is clear and safe for such a maneuver. When this has been completed, next check to see that a constant groundspeed is being maintained, but not one that is fast enough to lose ground cushion. This maneuver, due to its nature, will require maximum concentration on the part of the pilot. Finally, pick out some reference point to assist you in maintaining a definite direction. In the case of sideways flight, a point 90 degrees out from the cockpit in the direction of flight will serve best. In backwards flight, one directly out in front of the aircraft will work best. The only thing left is to tilt the cyclic stick in the direction you wish to fly. Coordinate collective and throttles to maintain altitude and rpms with the rudder controls to maintain heading.

The Hovering Turn

The hovering turn is a conventional helicopter maneuver that has proven to be quite useful in a number of circumstances. This maneuver teaches, more than most others, smooth coordination of all controls. While practicing, the maneuver is used to make 360 degree turns. In actual use, the turns may be stopped at any point.

To execute this maneuver, bring the ship into a hover state at a normal hover altitude. Once this is achieved, initiate the hovering turn by applying rudder pressure in a smooth easy manner in the direction you desire to turn. During this procedure, hold your altitude by the collective pitch, position over the hover spot by the cyclic pitch, and the turning action by pressure on the rudder pedal. During the turn, there will be noticed some tendency for the ship to whip at about 180 degrees around the turn. This whipping action can be anticipated and corrected for by rudder control at that point. This condition is more noticeable when executing this maneuver in the presence of wind. Winds of 10 mph can make it quite pronounced, and therefore, no attempt should be made to perform this maneuver when the winds are strong. Winds may be considered too strong when there is insufficient back cyclic control to hold the ship over the hover spot when it is headed downwind. As with all helicopter maneuvers, be wary of over-control.

Autorotation Landing

With the beginning of our discussion of autorotation, we are beginning the study of special flight techniques. While they are normal in the sense that the aerodynamics of flight make them possible and natural, they are nonetheless special in nature. These maneuvers are classified as special purpose and emergency techniques. This does not mean that they should not be practiced by every pilot, because they should. In fact, a proficiency in these maneuvers should be high on the priority list of *every* helicopter pilot. They not only provide the pilot with abilities that can save his life, they add to his versatility and capabilities as a pilot. Mastery of these maneuvers will provide the pilot with the ability to perform any special tasks that the rotary-wing aircraft are capable of, and increase his value both to himself and any prospective employer.

Autorotation is an emergency procedure, and may be considered much the same as a forced landing in a fixed-wing aircraft. Since this is an emergency procedure, it should be remembered that even the smallest error in judgement, mistake, or ineffective technique may prove to be *very* costly in life and property. There are two distinct types of autorotation landings, the running types and the flare-type. We will consider both, starting with the running type.

The only way to simulate this procedure is to practice it exactly as it would be executed in the case of that type of emergency. A power failure is the normal reason for this procedure. The simulation usually begins at an altitude above 300 feet and is ended within about 10 feet from the ground (Fig. 3-4).

To begin the maneuver, lower the collective stick to its full low position. As always, this should be done smoothly. It will be

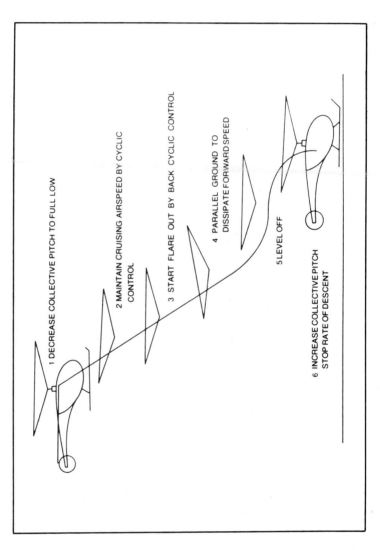

Fig. 3-4. Running landing.

1 DECREASE COLLECTIVE PITCH TO FULL LOW

2 MAINTAIN CRUISING AIRSPEED BY CYCLIC CONTROL

3 START FLARE OUT BY BACK CYCLIC CONTROL

4 PARALLEL GROUND TO DISSIPATE FORWARD SPEED

5 LEVEL OFF

6 INCREASE COLLECTIVE PITCH STOP RATE OF DESCENT

assumed that the ship is traveling at cruising speed up to this point; the engine is on and will remain on during this entire practice procedure. Remember, this is *simulated practice only*. As the pitch decreases, apply sufficient rudder to maintain the nose heading. When the collective stick is fully down, reduce throttle to a speed where the engine no longer is driving the rotor. This is called "splitting the needles" because the engine rpm is now less than the main rotor rpm as indicated on the dual needle tachometer. The helicopter is now in autorotation.

Once autorotation is begun, the airspeed and forward motion of the ship are controlled, as usual, by the cyclic stick. When practicing a running landing type of autorotation, airspeed should gradually be decreased as the descent progresses. When the helicopter is about 20 feet from the ground, the airspeed should still be approximately 15 mph. During the descent, the attitude of the aircraft should never be so nose-high that the tail assembly would hit the ground if that attitude were held until touchdown.

In simulated autorotations, a recovery is made by the use of collective stick action and throttle to stop the rate of descent at a safe altitude. This must be done smoothly, as any jerking action of the throttles or collective will bring about an extreme yawing of the nose from the sudden surge of torque from the engine.

If an actual touchdown is to be made, then at approximately 20 feet the ship should be returned to a level attitude by use of the cyclic control. This is extremely important because the helicopter must touchdown with its gear in a level attitude or a very dangerous situation can result.

A very careful evaluation of all conditions must be made prior to autorotation if an actual touchdown is to be made. Altitude, airspeed, CG location, gross weight, and wind conditions all are factors to be considered and evaluated prior to autorotation. All of these factors will have an effect on the way the pilot will handle the collective and cyclic controls during this emergency procedure. The closer any or all of these factors are to their critical limitations, the more precisely the pilot must respond. It will also be necessary to act more quickly on the collective stick in order to cushion the ship on touchdown. On a running landing, the collective pitch stick will be utilized at about five to ten feet from the ground. The more closely that any of the above named factors are to their critical limitations, as well as the faster the rate of descent, the more quickly the collective pitch stick must be employed. A running autorotation landing should result in the helicopter touching down at approximately 10 mph, and therefore, should only be utilized where a relatively smooth landing area is available.

The flare-type of autorotation is entered into in exactly the same way as the running landing. This procedure is far more difficult and requires a great deal more skill than does the former. The principal reason for this maneuver, over the running landing, is when the terrain is sufficiently rough and the running landing would be impractical. The chief difference in the two landings is that in the flare-type of autorotation procedure there is very little forward motion, if any, as compared to the running type of autorotation where there is usually about 10 mph forward groundspeed. It is this difference that makes the flare-type of maneuver practical in rough terrain (Fig. 3-5).

The major differences in executing the running and flare landing type of autorotation are as follows: normal cruising speed is maintained until the ship is within 75 feet of the ground. Here is where the flare-out procedure gets it name and is begun. This flare-out is accomplished by a smooth application of back pressure on the cyclic stick. The purpose of this action is to stop the descent of the helicopter completely by the time the ship is within 20 feet of the ground. This procedure also brings about a slowing of the ship while there is still some forward groundspeed. The pilot brings the ship into a level attitude with further action on the cyclic stick. It is at this point, if a simulation and no touchdown is to be attempted, that the recovery is made and is done exactly as for the running landing.

However, if an actual touchdown is to be made, it is here that the collective must be applied, and applied much more quickly than in the case of the running landing. This use of collective pitch stick has the effect of slowing the descent still further and cushioning the touchdown. There will be virtually no forward motion of any kind and will be almost like a hovering touchdown when properly executed.

Once again, the nearer the ship and surrounding conditions are to the critical point, the quicker and sharper must be the flare-out.

The Steep Approach

There are many instances when it may be necessary for the helicopter to be brought in in a very steep manner. Quite often there are tall obstacles, or the landing may be a very tight one which will require a landing that is almost vertical in execution.

Rescue work in difficult terrain, industrial applications, and helicopters located on top of buildings or in congested city areas, are just some of the reasons for such landings. One of the beauties of the helicopter is its ability to adapt itself to performing tasks under all such conditions, and hundreds more as well. It is in such difficult and limited operating circumstances that the helicopter can show off its great potential.

The steep approach landing may be considered a highly precision power glide approach to a specific spot, regardless of the surroundings. The steep approach is made in exactly the same way as the standard landing except that the angle of glide is steeper and far more precise. So precise, in fact, that the ship may be put down in a space only slightly larger than the area covered by the ship itself. This precision angle of glide can only be achieved by experience and a high degree of concentration by the pilot in the control and coordination of the collective and cyclic controls. Major corrections on the approach should only be instituted during the first one-third of the approach, and only minor ones thereafter. This is to avert the danger of coming in too low over high obstacles, or coming in vertically from too high an altitude to hit your landing spot.

The rate of descent is naturally much higher than in the standard landing; therefore, the collective pitch must be utilized sooner at the end of the approach. The groundspeed should be brought down to zero. Since the glide angle is much steeper, and the rate of descent much higher, considerably more power will be required at the end of the approach to make the transition from glide angle to hover. If the landing site is limited, great care will have to be exercised by the pilot in guiding his descent from obstacles on all sides (Fig. 3-6).

Maximum Performance Takeoffs

The same set of conditions that can necessitate the steep approach landing can and do require a maximum performance takeoff. When such a takeoff is required, the pilot must be thoroughly familiar with the capabilities and limitations of his ship. The pilot's best friend is his flight manual for that particular ship and is an invaluable tool here, as it is under so many conditions. Besides the capabilities and limitations of your ship, the pilot will have to know about, and take under consideration: wind velocity, air density, temperature, CG, and gross weight. These, and other

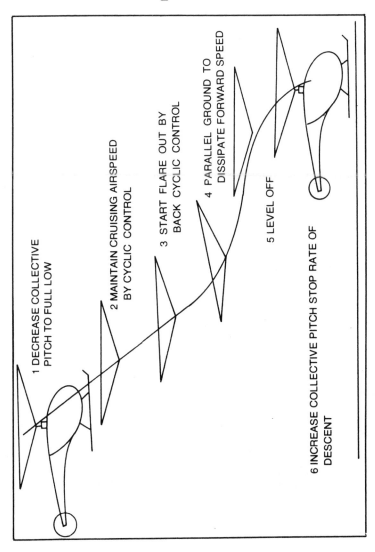

Fig. 3-5. Flare-type landing.

1 DECREASE COLLECTIVE
PITCH TO FULL LOW

2 MAINTAIN CRUISING AIRSPEED
BY CYCLIC CONTROL

3 START FLARE OUT BY
BACK CYCLIC CONTROL

4 PARALLEL GROUND TO
DISSIPATE FORWARD SPEED

5 LEVEL OFF

6 INCREASE COLLECTIVE PITCH STOP RATE OF
DESCENT

factors affecting technique and performance, are *absolutely essential* before attempting a maximum performance takeoff (Fig. 3-7).

The procedures for this type of takeoff are critical and must be followed explicitly, along with certain required observations, if the maneuver is to be safely and successfully accomplished. Increase collective pitch and throttle while watching the tachometer. Continue increasing both until the maximum red-line engine rpm is indicated on the tachometer and the ship becomes light on its landing gear. As the ship becomes airborne, increase the collective pitch and apply full throttle. When the helicopter becomes airborne it should be climbing and going forward at the same time in a very steep ascent angle. When climbing airspeed is achieved, come back on the cyclic stick slightly to prevent too much forward speed from decreasing the required angle of ascent. Continue with full power until the ship is safely clear of all obstacles, then power may be reduced and a normal, or standard rate of climb established.

The goal of this type of takeoff is to obtain a maximum altitude in a minimum amount of forward distance. The result will depend not only on the pilot's skill, but to a great extent on the performance and conditions outlined earlier. The less favorable these conditions, the shallower the angle of ascent will be. *Extreme* caution must be employed when climbing very steeply, for if airspeed is permitted to get too low, there is the ever-present danger that the helicopter may settle back to the ground. What could be even *more* dangerous is the possibility of a power failure at low altitude and airspeed which would place the craft into a *very* dangerous situation—one that would require a very high degree of skill to make a safe autorotation landing. Considerable caution and anticipatory judgment of any changing conditions and circumstances cannot be over emphasized.

The Fast Shallow Approach

The fast shallow approach is advisable when it is believed that there exists critical weather and sufficient landing space at a designated landing area. The glide angle is considerably shallower and the groundspeed much higher than in the standard approach and landing (Fig. 3-8).

Initiate an approach that will place the helicopter about five feet off the ground and 225 feet from the spot intended for touchdown. When the groundspeed has been reduced to 30 mph, place the craft in a level attitude; as the touchdown area approaches, use collective pitch as required to prevent a hard landing.

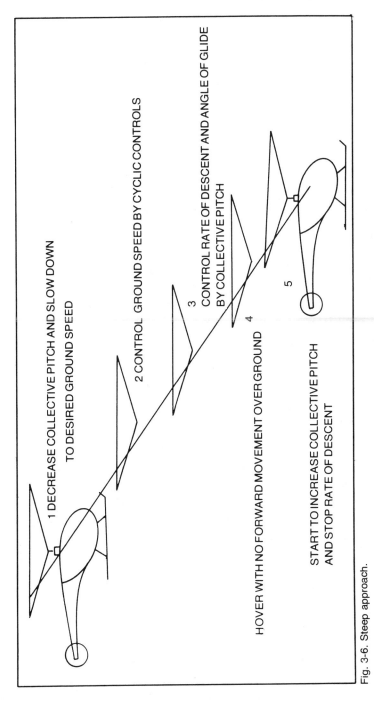

1 DECREASE COLLECTIVE PITCH AND SLOW DOWN TO DESIRED GROUND SPEED

2 CONTROL GROUND SPEED BY CYCLIC CONTROLS

3 CONTROL RATE OF DESCENT AND ANGLE OF GLIDE BY COLLECTIVE PITCH

4 HOVER WITH NO FORWARD MOVEMENT OVER GROUND

5 START TO INCREASE COLLECTIVE PITCH AND STOP RATE OF DESCENT

Fig. 3-6. Steep approach.

103

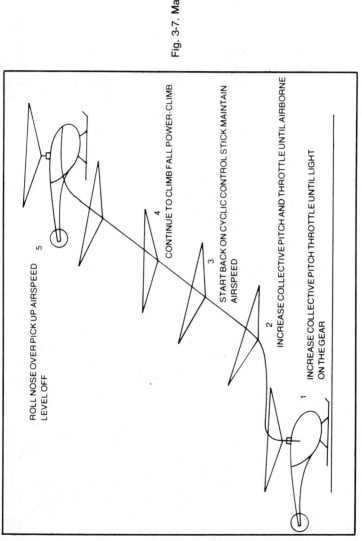

Fig. 3-7. Maximum performance takeoff.

5 ROLL NOSE OVER PICK UP AIRSPEED LEVEL OFF

4 CONTINUE TO CLIMB FALL POWER-CLIMB

3 START BACK ON CYCLIC CONTROL STICK MAINTAIN AIRSPEED

2 INCREASE COLLECTIVE PITCH AND THROTTLE UNTIL AIRBORNE

1 INCREASE COLLECTIVE PITCH THROTTLE UNTIL LIGHT ON THE GEAR

104

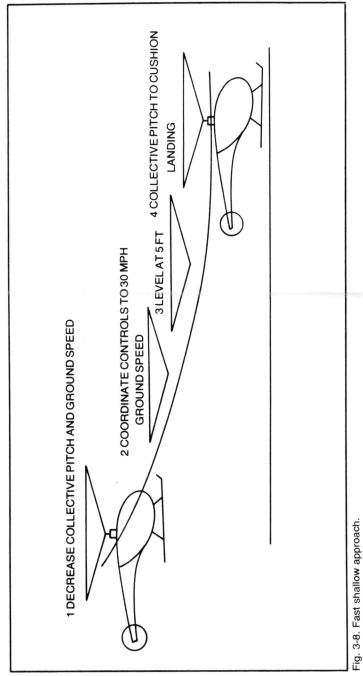

1 DECREASE COLLECTIVE PITCH AND GROUND SPEED

2 COORDINATE CONTROLS TO 30 MPH GROUND SPEED

3 LEVEL AT 5 FT

4 COLLECTIVE PITCH TO CUSHION LANDING

Fig. 3-8. Fast shallow approach.

This practical approach depends on translational lift for its success. Consequently, do not allow the groundspeed to get too low when nearing the touchdown point. The less groundspeed you have, the more collective stick prior to touchdown is to be avoided. It will probably result in a very hard landing.

The Running Rakeoff

The opposite of the fast shallow approach and landing is the running rakeoff. The reasons for its use are the same, with the exception that a heavy load and safety may dictate this type of takeoff, even though the weather is not critical. The requirements are much the same as for a shallow approach landing; a smooth, long area for the maneuver.

Begin this takeoff procedure by increasing collective pitch and throttle until the ship feels light on the landing gear. Next, tilt the cyclic stick forward to start the helicopter rolling. Maintain a straight path by keeping pressure on the rudder pedals as required.

No attempt should be made to have the helicopter become airborne until sufficient speed has been achieved to produce translational lift. Once this is achieved, a slight amount of back cyclic stick pressure, along with an increase of collective and throttles, will cause the ship to become airborne. Once airborne, increase power to full until a climbing airspeed has been reached. Until this time, no attempt should be made to climb. Failure to wait will probably result in the aircraft settling back onto the ground.

Rapid Deceleration

The maneuver is utilized whenever a quick stop in mid-air may be required and, is therefore, an excellent emergency procedure for the student pilot to practice. But there is much more to be gained from this practice. This is one of those maneuvers that are excellent for developing coordination (Fig. 3-9).

To practice rapid deceleration, an altitude of about 50 feet is desirable. The purpose of the maneuver is to remain at a constant altitude, heading, and rpm while, at the same time, slow the helicopter down to a desired groundspeed. The maneuver will put to the test the pilot's ability to coordinate simultaneous actions of the controls as few others can. Failure to properly coordinate simultaneous action of the controls will result in a change of altitude and an erratic varying of the rpm. To achieve rapid deceleration will require responsive coordinated action on the collective stick, throttles, cyclic stick and rudder at one time.

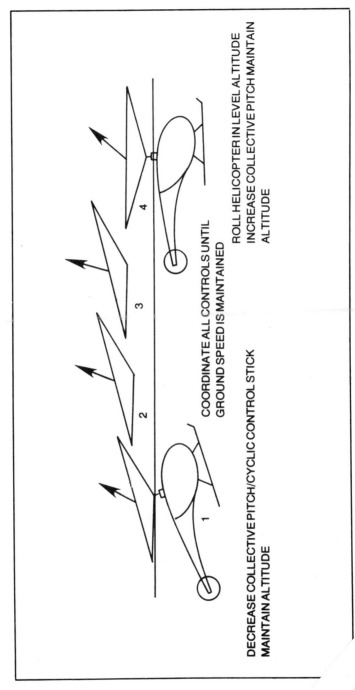

DECREASE COLLECTIVE PITCH/CYCLIC CONTROL STICK
MAINTAIN ALTITUDE

COORDINATE ALL CONTROLS UNTIL
GROUND SPEED IS MAINTAINED

ROLL HELICOPTER IN LEVEL ALTITUDE
INCREASE COLLECTIVE PITCH MAINTAIN
ALTITUDE

Rapid deceleration.

The maneuver is executed by decreasing collective pitch and coordinating the throttle to maintain a constant rpm. At the same time cyclic control must be eased back to maintain altitude. While this is being accomplished, it will be necessary to use a sufficient amount of rudder to hold a constant heading. The attitude of the aircraft will go nose-high and should be allowed to do so until the desired lower airspeed has been reached. The helicopter should never be allowed to go all the way to a zero groundspeed with the nose-high; such a condition would cause the ship to settle and the tail may strike the ground.

Once the ship's groundspeed has decreased the desired amount, the recovery should begin. This is achieved by leveling the ship with the cyclic stick and adjusting the collective stick and throttle to maintain altitude. At this point an opposite pressure on the rudder will be required to maintain the correct heading. A resumption of course and forward cruising speed may then be regained by tilting the cyclic stick in the desired direction, while adjusting the collective and throttles to maintain altitude and rpm.

Crosswind Conditions

Crosswind conditions can be most hazardous in a helicopter, and maneuvers should be kept at a minimum when encountered. If the pilot is in doubt about control limitations of the particular helicopter he is flying, no crosswind work should be undertaken. Again, the pilot's flight manual will be a source of information about the capabilities of the ship under these and other conditions as well. At any rate, no one but a seasoned pilot with good skills should attempt anything but the most basic flight in any kind of crosswinds.

One major consideration and problem during crosswind conditions is drift. Drift will result during almost any kind of flight maneuvering in a crosswind condition. Compensation is made by cyclic pressure in the opposite direction; however, a very high degree of coordination of all the controls will be required. Drift can be especially dangerous during either landings or takeoffs, and must be eliminated with cyclic stick control. If, for any reason, drift cannot be corrected during a takeoff the mission should, by all means, be aborted. During a landing attempt, if drift cannot be properly compensated for, every attempt should be made to find an alternative landing site before making any attempt to land with drift uncorrected.

Conclusions

There is possibly no greater thrill for many people than that enjoyed when flying a helicopter. The sheer joy of not only flying, but flying a type of aircraft that will allow the pilot to do just about anything in the air is beyond description. Rotary-wing flight has come of age, and the future is a bright one. We see almost daily an ever-increasing number of helicopters in the air performing an ever-increasing number of tasks. With the advent of truly successful auto-pilot systems, greater capabilities, more speed, and a larger variety of ships built to perform specific tasks, no one can predict just what the future holds. The competition between helicopter manufacturing companies has grown very intense, resulting in better ships at a greater variety of prices to meet the ever increasing needs of the user. There are few companies and even fewer industries that can match the record of helicopter manufacturers in their desire to produce better and safer products year after year.

While this chapter has provided an outline on how to fly a helicopter, this author hopes that no one is foolish enough to think that he needs nothing more to start attempting to fly a helicopter. Nothing could be further from the truth. The FAA, and other regulatory agencies in other countries, have set down requirements for the training of helicopter pilots; and have done so for good reason. To disobey or ignore these rules is in most countries a serious crime with stiff punishments. Violations can result in heavy fines and imprisonment *if the violater should survive his or her violation*.

The real intent of this chapter is to whet the appetite of the would-be student or transitional pilot to a point where they will want to enter into some formal type of helicopter flight training service or engineering training. This chapter, as well as the entire book, in intended as an academic supplement to that formal training, and nothing more.

Chapter 4

Construction, Design and Applications of the Helicopter: A Survey of the Industry

In this chapter I have chosen what I feel are a representative variety of the rotary-wing aircraft to display design, construction and engineering features of the modern helicopters. The manufacturers chosen were selected for their leading roles currently in the helicopter industry. It should not be misconstrued that they are the *only*, or even the so-called "best" rated helicopters in the world. There are many fine manufacturers of quality helicopters not represented in this book. This omission should *not* be taken in any way as a commentary on their products, nor as an endorsement of those who are represented. I have selected for presentation purposes only from those manufacturers with whose products I am familiar and feel confident to present in this work. Also, I felt comfortable with their technical staffs in obtaining much of the information contained in the book, and especially in this chapter. Contained in this chapter is a potpourri of designs, engineering features, sizes, shapes and types of helicopters. I believe that they will provide the reader with some idea of the variety of ships that are available to a helicopter-crazy public.

Bell Helicopter Company

The following information, photographs and illustrations were supplied and are presented through the courtesy of Bell Helicopter Textron, Division of Textron, Inc.

Bell Helicopter Textron of Fort Worth, Texas, is the largest division of Textron Inc. It has produced and sold more military and

110

commercial helicopters in a worldwide market than all other manufacturers combined.

The firm has been an integral part of the Forth Worth-Dallas industrial community since 1951 when its rotary-wing design, development and production activities were moved to Texas from Buffalo, New York.

All company manufacturing facilities are located in the Greater Fort Worth area except for one at Amarillo, Texas. The Greater Fort Worth operations utilize more than 2,600,000 square feet of enclosed space on more than 1,160 acres of land.

Bell had produced 25,000 helicopters for its military and commercial customers. These aircraft are in operation in a wide variety of missions in virtually every free world country.

Current production commercial helicopters include the six to ten-place Model 222, the five-place, turbine-powered Model 206B Jet Ranger-III, the 12 to 15-place turbine Model 205A-1, the twin-turbine 212, the seven-place, light-turbine 206L-1 Long Ranger-II and the 214 Big Lifter which can carry 7,000 pounds (3,175 kg) on the hook. Under development are the 214ST Super Transport, which seats up to 19 persons and Model 412, a four-bladed variant of the twin-turbine 212.

Military helicopters currently in production include the UH-1 Huey series in both single-engine and twin-engine versions and improved versions of the single and twin-engine AH-1 Cobra armed helicopter series.

Another key project is Bell's work on the XV-15 tilt rotor research aircraft. The program stems from a joint contract with NASA and the U. S. Army Research and Technology Laboratories (AVRADCOM) to design, manufacture and test two VTOL aircraft. The XV-15's first full conversion to the airplane mode was made on July 24, 1979 by Aircraft No. 2. Since then it has attained forward flight speeds of more than 300 miles per hour. Additional funding to accelerate and expand the test effort has been provided to the program by the U. S. Navy (Fig. 4-1).

Bell helicopters also are built under license by Costruzioni Aeronautiche Giovanni Augusta of Milan, Italy and Mitsui & Co.

Model 205A. The Bell 205A is a 15-place single turbine engine powered medium helicopter for corporate and utility use. See Fig. 4-2.

Model 214B. Also known as *the "Big Lifter"* this is a 16-place single-engine turbine powered medium helicopter for utility and corporate use. See Fig. 5-3.

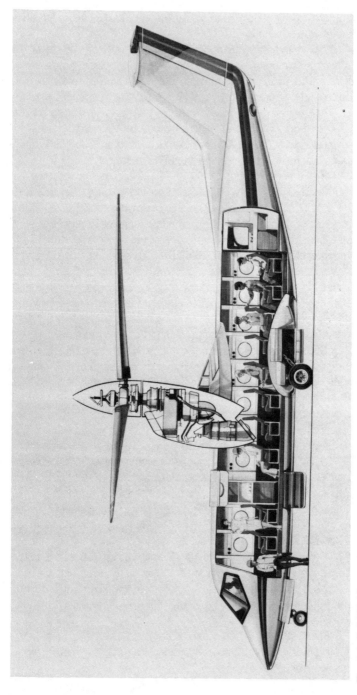

Fig. 4-1. Bell XV-15.

Fig. 4-2. Bell 205A.

Model 212. This is a twin turbine powered 15-place category helicopter for corporate and utility operations. See Fig. 4-4.

Model 214ST. The "ST" stands for *Supertransport*, a powerful new 18-place, twin turbine helicopter that will be a most productive, most effective medium utility workhorse serving petroleum and construction industry needs through the decade of the '80s. Not only will the 214ST transport people (work crews, inspection teams, supervisory personnel) long distances quickly, but it can haul great amounts of cargo over roadless terrain or open oceans to hard-to-reach job sites, in inclement weather, day and night.

The Bell 214ST's load carrying capability exceeds that of any other comparably sized helicopter. This is a tremendous advantage

Fig. 4-3. Bell 214B "Big Lifter."

Fig. 4-4. Bell 212.

when operating in the hot climates and high altitudes for which it was designed.

Speaking of design, the 214ST has twin advanced-technology General Electric turbines, each delivering 1,625 shp, twin hydraulic systems, and twin electrical systems. Many components, such as the fiberglass rotor blades, have been proven in FAA certified Bell helicopters. Second generation Noda-Matic suspension provides a smoother, quieter, more comfortable passenger environment.

The Bell 214ST has been engineered for exceptional multimission capability. It can do a variety of jobs, and do them well.

The 18-place 214ST is ideal for carrying entire crews or other personnel out to distant rigs and back. It has an operating radius of over 200 NM (370 KM). Externally, the 214ST can lift and move over three tons, even in hot climates or high altitudes. What's more, achieving the ON CONDITION TBO goal will keep the

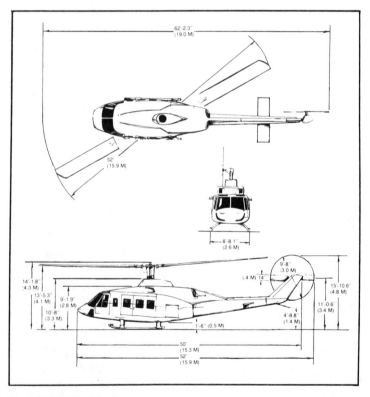

Fig. 4-5. Bell 214ST, general arrangement.

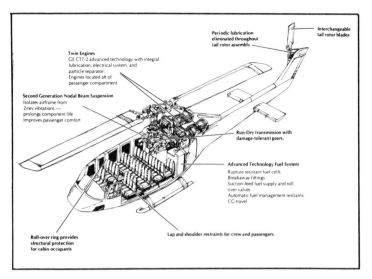

Fig. 4-6. Bell 214ST, cutaway view.

214ST on the job longer. Within its spacious cabin, the 214ST can hold 316 cubic feet ($9m^3$) of cargo—up to 6,000 pounds (2722 Kg) of drilling equipment, machine parts, supplies or whatever can be transported easily.

For a close look, see Figs. 4-5 through 4-7, and Table 4-1.

Bell 412. The Bell 412 is a powerful new 15-place helicopter with two PT6T-3B Pratt & Whitney turbines and a new advanced design four-bladed rotor system (Figs. 4-8 through 4-12).

Fig. 4-7. Bell 214ST cockpit.

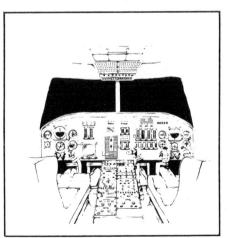

Table 4-1. Bell 214ST Performance.

	UNITS			
	LB	12500	14500	16500
TAKEOFF GROSS WEIGHT	KG	5670	6577	7484
ICE HOVER CEILING				
	FT	18100	14600	11500
Standard Day	M	5517	4450	3505
	FT	16600	12700	9100
Standard Day + 20°C	M	5060	3871	2774
OGE HOVER CEILING				
	FT	14800	11200	3900
Standard Day	M	4511	3414	1189
	FT	12900	8700	1600
Standard Day + 20°C	M	3932	2652	488
RANGE				
4000 ft., Standard Day				
VFR, Internal Fuel,	NM	515	484	451
No Reserves	KM	954	896	835
Average Long Range	KT	141	141	140
Cruise Speed	KM/HR	261	261	259
SINGLE ENGINE SERVICE CEILING (30 MIN POWER)				
	FT	15100	11600	8200
Standard Day	M	4602	3536	2499
	FT	13200	9300	5300
Standard Day + 20°C	M	4023	2835	1615
CRUISE SPEED (MAXIMUM CONTINUOUS POWER)				
	KT	153	148	142
Sea Level, Standard Day	KM/HR	283	274	263
	KT	155	150	140
4000 Ft (1200 M) Standard Day	KM/HR	287	278	259

With a cruise speed of 130 knots and an offshore range of up to 350 nautical miles, the 412 is a particularly desirable aircraft for the petroleum industry, providing a fast, efficient crew change transport capability into the 1980s and beyond.

More than 5,000 pound (2268 kilograms) internal useful load capacity, plus a cabin with wide doors for easy loading, make the new 412 ideal for rough terrain construction tasks, and to supply remote area job sites. For increased work versatility, it boasts exceptional hot climate-high altitude operating characteristics.

For increased availability, the 412 will be IFR certified for night flight and inclement weather conditions.

We are grateful to Bell Helicopter Textron for their excellent and extensive materials. Viewing their fine fleet of versatile aircraft from the past, present and future is like viewing the history and future of the helicopter itself. Their willingness to share construction details and applications with our readers is characteristic of this company's interest in the future and future helicopter people as well.

Boeing Vertol Helicopters

The following information, photographs and illustrations were supplied and are presented through the courtesy of the Boeing Vertol Company, Division of Boeing Company.

The Boeing Company, Seattle, Washington, recognized throughout the world as the leader in commercial jet transports,

Fig. 4-8. Bell 412.

119

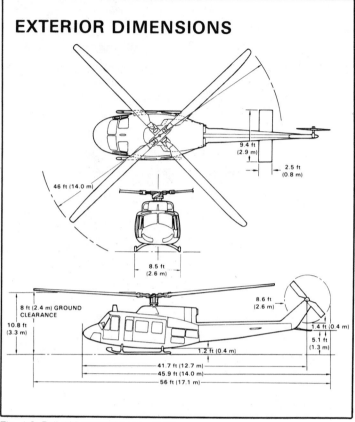

EXTERIOR DIMENSIONS

9.4 ft (2.9 m)

2.5 ft (0.8 m)

46 ft (14.0 m)

8.5 ft (2.6 m)

8 ft (2.4 m) GROUND CLEARANCE

10.8 ft (3.3 m)

8.6 ft (2.6 m)

1.4 ft (0.4 m)

5.1 ft (1.3 m)

1.2 ft (0.4 m)

41.7 ft (12.7 m)

45.9 ft (14.0 m)

56 ft (17.1 m)

Fig. 4-9. Bell 412 general arrangement.

entered the helicopter field in 1960 with the acquisition of Vertol Aircraft Corporation in suburban Philadelphia, Pennsylvania. Since its founding in 1943, Vertol has produced and delivered over 2,500 tandem-rotor helicopters for the U. S. military service and many foreign nations.

During the mid-1940s, the company designed and developed the world's first tandem-rotor transport helicopter, the SHRP-1. The HRP series helicopters were the first to demonstrate the superiority of the tandem-rotor configuration for transporting heavy loads over long distances. During the ensuing years, the company built more 1,000 piston-powered tandem-rotor helicopters for military forces in the U. S. and overseas. Model designations included the HUP (UH-25), the H-21, YF-16, Vertol 42, 43 and 44.

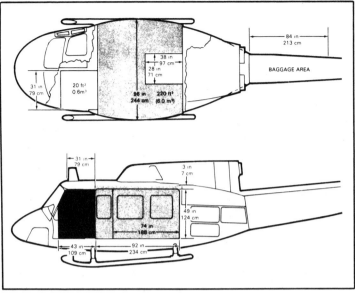

Fig. 4-10. Bell 412 interior dimensions.

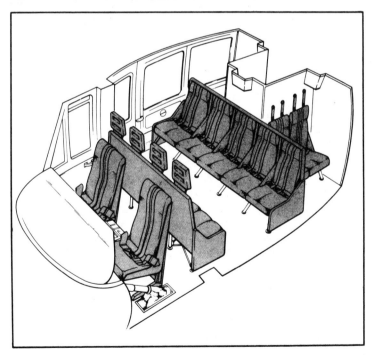

Fig. 4-11. Bell 412 standard seating.

121

With the coming of the "jet age" during the late 1950s, the company began efforts to design a new generation of turbine-powered helicopters.

During the 1960s, the fleet of Boeing Vertol turbine-powered helicopters became operational. The Model 107, a 25-passenger aircraft, entered commercial airline service. A military version of the aircraft, the CH-46 "Sea Knight," was selected by the U. S. Marine Corps for its assault and transport missions. The CH-47 Chinook, a large tandem-rotor helicopter, capable of carrying 44 combat-equipped troops, was order by the U. S. Army.

Today, Boeing Vertol's CH-47 Chinooks provide the U. S. Army and military forces in 10 other nations with medium-lift uses, the aircraft has received worldwide recognition for its "life-saving" role in civil disasters such as floods, earthquakes and fires.

H-46 helicopters are in service with the U. S. Navy and Marine Corps and with several foreign countries. Commercial Model 107s are engaged in logging, power line installation, firefighting and other industrial uses in the U. S. and overseas.

In 1978, Boeing Vertol launched its 234 Commercial Chinook program when British Airways Helicopters (BAH) placed an initial order for the aircraft.

The 234 Chinook has the largest passenger capacity and cargo carrying capabilities of any commercial helicopter now available. It can carry 44 passenger non-stop over a distance of 550 nautical miles with reserves and it can externally lift 28,000 pounds of cargo. Internally the 234 Chinook can carry loads as heavy as 20,000 pounds. The aircraft has a cruise speed of 140 knots.

Boeing Commercial Airplane Company has selected Vertol to build the fixed leading edge for the wings of the new 757 and 767 airplanes. Vertol is also building parts and assemblies for other models of Boeing jet transports including the E3A and C-135 (Air Force designations for the 707), 727, 737 and 747.

Vertol 76. This experimental aircraft, pioneered in 1957, was the first tilt-wing VTOL ever built (Fig. 4-13). It was developed for the U. S. Army and the Office of Naval Research as the Vertol 76 (VZ-2), the first tilt-wing to go through conversion from vertical flight to horizontal and back again. The first successful complete conversion flight was July 15, 1958.

The entire wing and both rotor/propellers can be titled to a vertical position, thus enabling the 76 to take off and land like a helicopter. The aircraft transitions from hover to forward flight as the wing and rotor/propellers are titled forward to the horizontal

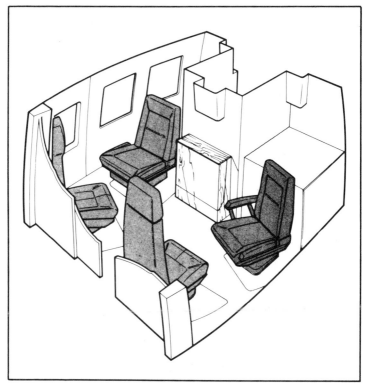

Fig. 4-12. Bell 412 luxury seating.

position. The 76 then flies like a fixed-wing aircraft. Consequently, it has unusual potential for close support under terrain conditions that would nullify the effectiveness of a less versatile aircraft.

The Vertol 76 successfully completed an extensive three-year flight test program and underwent flight tests of an advanced wing configuration. These and similar test programs led to a number of state-of-the-art breakthroughs in tilt-wing technology. In 1965, the Vertol 76 was retired to take its place in history with the other aviation firsts at the Smithsonian Institute Museum in Washington, D.C.

HUP Series. The Navy Bureau of Aeronautics wrote requirements in 1945 for a high-performance utility helicopter to operate from aircraft carriers, battleships, and cruisers. The competition for this type was won by the tandem-rotor HUP, or as it was then known, the XHJP-1.

The prototype XHJP-1 had won a Navy production contract in competition with a single-rotor helicopter built in identical operational specifications. It was the first helicopter to incorporate overlapping tandem-rotor blades and prove the all-around advantages of this configuration.

The HUP, now designated the UH-25 retriever by the Navy, is a six-place, single-engine rescue and utility helicopter. The fuselage is of all-metal, semimonocoque construction with a conventional fixed landing gear. The overlapped tandem design provides a compact fuselage and rotor system, permitting the HUP to be handled on any aircraft carrier elevator without folding the blades and on any cruiser elevator with blades folded. The mission of the HUP is shipbased rescue, observation and utility, personnel and cargo transport.

The HUP-2 was the first production helicopter to be equipped with an auto-pilot which permits "hands off" flying. A total of 339 HUP type helicopters were delivered to the U. S. Navy, the U. S. Army (H-25s), the Royal Canadian Navy, and the French Navy. The Army's H-25 was known as the "Army Mule" and doubled as a troop carrier and flying ambulance (Fig. 4-14).

An example of the HUP's versatility was the performance of a single U. S. Navy squadron of twelve HUP-2s during rescue and relief operations at Tampico, Mexico, after the area had been badly damaged by a hurricane. In 2,298 day sorties and 88 night sorties, a total of 184,037 pounds of food was delivered to Mexican flood victims; 81 medical teams were transported together with 1,867 pounds of medical supplies. In a single day 2,280 persons were evacuated—1,425 of them rescued by hoist. One pilot transported 21 persons—a remarkable achievement for a six-place helicopter.

H-16 Series. Originally selected by the United States Air Force as a long-range transport helicopter, the YH-16 also incorporated the United States Marine Corps and United States Army Field Force characteristics for an assault transport helicopter capable of transporting large quantities of troops and quipment inot critical combat areas. It was the largest helicopter in the world at the time, with space provisions for 40 troops or seven tons of cargo in its 2,250-cubic foot cabin.

Two of these big experimental helicopters were built for the USAF: the YH-16 Transporter, test flown in 1953, and powered with two reciprocating engines delivering a total of 3,600-horsepower, and the YH-16A Turbo Transporter, powered with two Allison YT38 turbines geared directly to the 82-foot diameter rotors (Fig. 4-15). The first public showing of the latter took place at Philadelphia's International Airport in December 1955.

Fig. 4-13. Boeing Vertol 76.

Fig. 4-14. Boeing HUP.

Fig. 4-15. Boeing H-16.

The YH-16A unofficially broke the existing helicopter record in 1956 with a speed of 166 miles per hour. Its service ceiling was over 18,000 feet. Data gathered from ground and flight tests of the YH-16A were instrumental in the further development of large turbine-powered, tandem-rotor helicopters.

CH-21 Series. When the first YH-21, now designated CH-21, was delivered to the United States Air Force in 1953 it was immediately placed into rescue service in the Arctic without the benefit of any formal service evaluation of its performance. This "beefed up" version of the HRP-2, which had won the USAF competition for a long-range rescue helicopter, had to prove its reliability and ruggedness under the severest conditions as an operational aircraft (Fig. 4-16).

Because of its excellent performance, its winterization features which permitted operation at temperatures as low as minus 65°F, and its capability of being routinely maintained under the same severe conditions, the CH-21A was given additional duties by the Air Force as a cargo and personnel transport in the most northern areas of Alaska, Canada, and Greenland. In support of the DEW Line, CH-21Bs were used as the prime support of the Texas Tower radar stations situated out in the Atlantic, off the coast of the United States.

The Royal Canadian Air Force employed CH-21 type helicopters in active support of the Mid-Canada Radar Line before turning the job and the helicopters over to Spartan Air Service. The U. S. Army uses the CH-21C Shawnee as a tactical and logistical support vehicle.

The CH-21C and an export model designated the Vertol 43 have both received their baptism under fire, serving with distinction in combat with the French Army in Algeria and, more recently, achieved a notable combat record with U. S. Army Military Assistance Groups serving with Government forces fighting Communist Viet Cong guerrillas in the jungles, mountains, and rice paddies of South Vietnam. These helicopters have proven to be surprisingly invulnerable to small arms ground fire, suffering as many as eight bullet hits in a single blade without causing the mission to be aborted.

An experimental model, powered with twin T53 turbine engines, was the forerunner of the turbine-powered transports. This was designated the Vertol 105. Another twin-turbine installation, using T58s, was developed and flown under a U. S. Navy contract. This helicopter was designated the CH-21D.

Fig. 4-16. Boeing CH-21.

The Vertol 44 is an improved, FAA-certified CH-21 type helicopter for military and commercial operations. Some of the prime differences between the 44 and the H-21C are: all-metal rotor blades, increased power, reduced drag, and a roll rate damper stability device which resulted in improved flying qualities.

The CH-21's have served as air rescue helicopters with the RCAF and USAF; as utility transports with the U. S. Army and German Army; on ASW and minesweeping operations with the Royal Swedish Navy and the French Navy.

The commercial version, the 44B, was operated by New York Airways, Sabena Belgian World Airlines, and Spartan Air Service, as well as in the petroleum and construction industry.

This outstanding series of helicopters has amassed a truly remarkable record of service and versatility since the first CH-21 was delivered to the USAF in 1953.

HRP Series. The SHRP-X Dogship was the first helicopter produced under the military contract. Designed and built in record time for the U. S. Navy in March 1945, it not only was the first successful tandem-rotor helicopter but also the largest helicopter to fly successfully at the time (Fig. 4-17). Two XHRP-1s quickly followed and served as static/dynamic and flight test articles. From these helicopters the basic principles of control were developed for the subsequent HRP-1, on which extensive flight test program was conducted.

The HRP-1 was ten-place helicopter powered by a 600-horsepower Pratt & Whitney R-1340 engine. Twenty aircraft were constructed under a Navy contract, and deliveries were completed in 1948. These helicopters performed numerous rescue misssions with both the Navy and the Coast Guard. Using the HRP-1, rescues and medical missions up to 90 miles at sea were successfully completed by the U. S. Coast Guard.

The HRP-2, five of which were produced, was an all-metal fuselage version of the HRP-1, with a number of refinements and modifications.

The HRP series helicopters were the first to demonstrate the towing capability of VTOL aircraft, and to establish the superiority of the tandem-rotor configuration for this operation. As mine sweepers, their speed was comparable with that of surface vessels, without the inherent danger of striking mines. Their ten-passenger capacity ushered in the era of transport helicopter operations.

The Boeing Military Chinook. The Chinook, which has been in continuous production since 1961, has proven record of reliable, rugged service under the most rigorous conditions around the world.

The Chinook has been improved continually as technology has advanced. The current version of the legendary Chinook, the CH-47 is everything its predecessors were with the experience of over 1,500,000 flight hours included.

It is a twin-engine, tandem-rotor, all-weather helicopter with a uniquely efficient fuselage. It can carry more cargo and passengers than any other helicopter in the free world. The CH-47 has a loading ramp and external cargo hooks with can carry loads up to 28,000 pounds (12,700 kg). The tandem-rotor design permits an internal load capability of over 27,000 pounds (12,250 kg). With the installation of auxiliary fuel tanks, the Chinook has a range of 1080 nautical miles (2,000 km), and can cruise at a speed of 165 knots.

Many of the over 900 Chinooks built fly for foreign nations around the globe. It is ideally suited for its international role. It is amphibious for use in rescue, relief and exploration roles; it is built to withstand the dust of deserts and moisture of jungles; it is equally at home in the heat of the equator and the cold of the arctic. With its high altitude capability, the Chinook is perfect for rugged, mountainous terrain.

The U. S. Army currently has a program for modernizing their CH-47A, B and C model helicopters to convert them to an improved CH-47D configuration. This decision by the U. S. Army to modernize its Chinook fleet, rather than replace it, attests to the superior performance of the Chinook. It assures that the Boeing-built helicopter will be in service through the 1990s.

Fig. 4-17. Boeing HRP.

Recent sales of military Chinooks include 33 for the United Kingdom's Royal Air Force, eight for the U. S. Army, three for the Argentine Air Force and two for the Argentine Army.

Armed/Armored Chinook. In later 1965, the first Armed/Armored Chinook was officially rolled out and testing was begun. The Armed/Armored Chinook used its payload capability to advantage by mounting an extensive array of armament, as well as armor to protect the crew and vital parts of the aircraft against heavy caliber ground fire (Fig. 4-18).

Mounted on the nose was an M-5 40mm automatic grenade launcher. This turret-mounted weapon was controlled by the copilot, who was able to cover an extensive area on either side of the flight path. Complementing this nose turret, pylons on each side of the aircraft carried fixed forward-firing weapons including a 20mm gun and either one 19-round 2.75 inch rocket pod, or a 7.62mm high-rate-of-fire minigun.

The flanks of the aircraft were protected by four gunners stationed two to either side of the cabin. Each of these gunners was provided with either a 7.62mm or 50 caliber machine gun on flexible mounts. Another gunner was stationed aft with the same type weapons mounted on the rear loading ramp. From this vantage point, the gunner could protect the aircraft from ground fire after the aircraft had passed, a capability not present in previous armed helicopters. This aircraft carried a ton of expendable munitions.

The Armed/Armored Chinook was provided with a new type of steel armor plate which was built into the crew seats and protected their torsos. Other steel plates protected components of the aircraft. The rugged components of the Chinook and extensive

Fib. 4-18. Boeing Armed/Armored Chinook.

dualization of systems, combined with over a ton of armor plate, assured a high degree of survivability for the aircraft.

Model 107-II (H-46 Sea Knight). The Boeing 106-II (U. S. military Sea Knight) is a fully-operational, medium transport helicopter. It is currently being used for both military and civil operations in the United States, Canada, Sweden and Japan. Over 600 107-IIs were manufactured in the 1965-1971 time period. Production of the 107-II continues at Kawasaki Heavy Industries, Ltd. under license from Boeing Vertol. Its tandem-rotor design provides optimum flight stability and permits considerable flexibility in carrying personnel and cargo. It can carry a payload of over 7,000 pounds (3150 kg), fly at 140 knots (252 kilometers) per hour, and has a water-landing and takeoff capability.

The U. S. Marine Corps version, designated the CH-46 Sea Knight, is an assault transport used to carry troops, fuel and supplies (Fig. 4-19). The U. S. Navy UH-46 is used mainly for the transfer of supplies between ships at sea and general utility. The HH-46 is utilized for shore-based search and rescue (SAR).

In a modification program spanning the next four years, the U. S. Marines are updating their Sea Knight fleet. The changes for the CH-46 include the installation of uprated T58-GE-16 engines, pilot and copilot crash attenuating seats, crash and combat-resistant fuel system and improved rescue system.

Boeing Vertol also has a contract from the Naval Air System Command to produce fiberglass rotor blades to replace the metal rotor blades in the CH-46 fleet. Boeing Vertol flight testing of the fiberglass rotor blades was completed in 1977, and Navy evaluation successfully completed early in 1978. A total production program of approximately 3,000 fiberglass rotor blades is planned.

Together, modernization and fiberglass rotor blade programs will serve to keep the CH-46 a first-line aircraft through the next decade.

In the area of commercial helicopter operations, Columbia Helicopters, Inc. of Aurora, Oregon, operates a fleet of 11 107-IIs. Columbia uses the aircraft for a variety of utility missions such a logging, power line construction and offshore oil operations.

CH-47 Modernization Program. The CH-47 Modernization Program is designed to meet the U. S. Army's continuing medium-lift helicopter (MLH) needs at the lowest possible cost and risk. This effort began in 1976 when the Boeing Vertol Company was awarded a full-scale engineering development contract by the U. S. Army to remanufacture three earlier model tandem-rotor Chinook helicopters, one A, one B and one C model, to new D (Delta) model prototypes. The contract also enabled Boeing Vertol to design, develop, test and qualify new component systems for the Delta prototypes (Fig. 4-20).

Production has now been completed on the three Delta prototypes, each of which is involved in flight testing at present. All have successfully completed Developmental Test (D.T.) activity, which is the second major phase of the flight test program. During D.T., which took place at the U. S. Army's Aviation Center at Fort

Fib. 4-19. Boeing CH46.

Rucker, Alabama, the B and C Chinook prototypes collectively flew 341 test hours, compared to a required objective of 280 flight test hours. By successfully meeting the required flight test hours, as well as other test goals, D.T. was completed on schedule.

D. T. involves both Army and Boeing Vertol tests to verify the aircraft's new components and that required technical objectives are attainable.

Two of the three prototypes are now undergoing Operational Testing (O.T.) at Fort Campbell, Kentucky. The third prototype, meanwhile, has just returned to Boeing Vertol for additional flight testing in Philadelphia, Pennsylvania, from Minneapolis, Minnesota, where it underwent two months of ice/cold weather testing.

O.T. involves Army testing to see if the aircraft meets its RAM characteristics (reliability, availability and maintainability) as well as its performance requirements when supported and operated by any Army unit. The two prototypes involved in O.T. at Fort Campbell are, in a sense, returning home. The aircraft, former B and C model Chinooks, were previously used by the 101st Airborne Division which is stationed at Fort Campbell.

Production for the modernization program involves stripping the aircraft to their frames and then rebuilding them with their improved systems. New components and technology incorporated into the D model will provide the Army with a medium-lift helicopter fleet containing 150 percent of the current productivity, while requiring 20 percent less in direct operating costs. New components and systems in the D model include:

☐ Improved transmission with 7500 SHP rating;
☐ Redundant and improved electrical systems;
☐ Fiberglass rotor blades;
☐ Lycoming T55-L-712 engines with emergency power;
☐ Integral lubrication and cooling for transmission systems;
☐ Modularized hydraulic systems;
☐ Triple cargo hook suspension system;
☐ Advanced flight control system;
☐ Improved avionics equipment;
☐ Redesigned cockpit configuration to reduce pilot workload.

The rollout for the first prototype took place in March, 1979, with the first flight taking place two months later in May. Both events were four months ahead of schedule. Each of the prototypes

Fig. 4-20. Boeing CH47D prototypes.

has logged over 3500 flight hours and was involved in combat operations in Vietnam.

Army plans call for 361 earlier model Chinooks to be remanufactured under this program, over a 10-12 year timespan, as well as additional new production CH-47D's to meet the Army's continuing MLH needs.

Boeing 234 Chinook. Boeing Vertol Company launched its 234 Commercial Chinook program in November of 1978 when British Airways Helicopters (BAH) placed an order for three of the aircraft (Fig. 4-21). Since then, BAH has announced orders for three additional 234 Chinooks.

The 234 Chinook has the largest passenger capacity and cargo carrying capabilities of any commercial helicopter currently available. It can carry 44 passengers non-stop over a distance of 550 nautical miles with reserves and it can externally lift 28,000 pounds of cargo. Internally the 234 Chinook can carry loads as heavy as 20,000 pounds. The aircraft has a cruise speed of 140 knots.

The 234 Chinook is also versatile. It can be configured to carry passengers, large cargo loads, or both at the same time.

Fig. 4-21. Boeing 234.

The passenger version Chinook (designated the long-range version, LR) has a maximum gross weight capability of 47,000 pounds. The interior design is similar to that found on the company's commercial airplanes (Fig. 4-22). The interior contains the following passenger-oriented comfort features: pleasant, eye appealing interior design; roomy, comfortable seats; individual service units; complete lavatory facilities; overhead baggage compartments; passenger windows; pleasant lighting conditions, stereo headphones; and a food or beverage galley.

With its 51,000 pound gross weight capacity, the utility version 234 Chinook, or UT as it is called, does the rugged, heavy lifting chores. Heavy objects this aircraft can lift include tractors, pipelines, towers, hugh bulk containers and, if necessary, another helicopter the size of a Chinook.

Since the 234 Chinook is a derivative of the famed Boeing CH-47 family of military Chinooks, it contains many of the same safety features which have allowed the Chinook fleet to log more than 1.6 million flight hours since 1962 with an outstanding safety record. Many of these hours have been logged under the most severe and dangerous of all conditions—hostile combat operations.

All of these factors—payload capability, versatility and safety—make the Boeing 234 Chinook ideal for use in today's civilian helicopter market, which has a variety of needs for an aircraft with the characteristics of the 234.

There are currently five major uses proposed for the aircraft by helicopter operators. These include support for offshore oil operations; logging; remote source development (land-based mining or ocean-based exploration, etc.); utility construction; and short-to-medium haul passenger transportation.

Fig. 4-22. Boeing 234 interior.

Most of these uses are dictated by the world's need to recover natural resources, many of which are located in remote and inaccessible areas, or in ocean areas distant from land.

As the world's search for offshore oil intensifies due to the increasing uncertainty over the availability of land-based petroleum supplies, the search for offshore oil is now being focused around the world. This includes such areas as the Gulf of Mexico, the North Sea, the Beaufort Sea and the coasts of South America and Australia. In order to efficiently and safely transport workers and cargo to the rigs, some of which are hundreds of miles from shore, a helicopter is needed that can swiftly carry large payloads over long distances.

For example, BAH plans to fly both passengers and priority cargo in its recently purchased 234 Chinooks to North Sea platforms operated by Shell and Exxon.

Another reason why the 234 is the ideal helicopter for offshore oil support, especially in an area such as the North Sea, is that it can comfortably, safely and economically fly passengers to and from the rigs despite severe weather conditions.

The 234 also meets stringent British CAA ditching requirements up to Sea State seven (30 foot wave heights). With the large fuel pods on either side of the aircraft, the Chinook becomes inherently stable in rough seas.

The Chinook with its long range capability will provide increased productivity for offshore oil operations in the North Sea. For example, no longer will BAH have to initially load workers or cargo onto fixed-wing aircraft for flight from Aberdeen, Scotland, to Sumburgh in the Shetland Isles, where workers are currently boarding helicopters for final sea-based destinations. Instead, the 234 Chinook will fly the workers directly to their final destination—the rigs. This saves overtime and gets the workers on the job even in weather that prevents fixed-wing aircraft from operating. Moreover, a single Chinook is able to do the job of three or four smaller helicopters.

Other uses are also available for the 234 Chinook. Because of the world's increasing need for wood products, the 234 will prove invaluable in helping to harvest timber, especially in those areas which are hard to reach via conventional surface transportation modes. Already Columbia Helicopters of Portland, Oregon, is using an earlier Boeing Vertol design tandem-rotor helicopter, the 107-II, to harvest difficult-to-reach timber in the Pacific Northwest. During 1978 the firm logged more than 175 million board feet of timber—enough wood to build 25,000 homes.

The Chinook will also prove valuable in the construction of long electrical power lines where it is difficult to transport heavy construction equipment without adversely affecting the environment.

Because of its large payload capability, the 234 will also be able to assist in developing the earth's resources in remote and inaccessible areas. For example, it can participate in mining operations in mountainous areas, or, in jungle regions which are impossible to reach via surface roads. It operates even in ocean farming/mining activities which require a large payload capability.

Finally, because of the world's need for more efficient passenger transportation, the 234 Chinook is being considered for flying passengers from one city center to another within a 200-mile radius.

It is the latest advanced technology which gives the 234 Chinook such commercial promise. The following is a list of such technology:

☐ Fiberglass composite rotor blades;

☐ Redundant auxiliary lubrication systems and strengthened power train gears;

☐ Advanced avionics, including dual flight control system;

☐ A triple-cargo hook suspension system;

☐ Oil-cooled generators, swaged hydraulic fittings, electrical back generators and jamproof flight control actuators;

☐ Large fuel cells (which allow the aircraft to meet stringent British government emergency flotation requirements);

☐ A crashworthy fuel system;

☐ Avco-Lycoming engines, among other features.

The interior design of the aircraft also furthers its commercial promise. It features a wide interior fuselage which contains more than 1,449 cubic feet of usable storage volume. An additional 227 cubic feet of storage is located in the area over the drive-in ramp, which can be used for baggage storage.

The 234 Chinook is built with maintenance in mind. In this regard it is nearly a self-sufficient vehicle. All integral work platforms are accessible by built-in steps and handholds. An onboard auxiliary power unit eliminates the need for external support equipment. The fiberglass blades, which are noncorrosive and difficult to damage, require a minimum of maintenance. The AL-4412 engines are podded for ease of access and engine rework when required.

Rollout and first flight of the 234 Chinook are scheduled to take place in mid-1980. Following FAA and CAA certification, the aircraft is expected to be in revenue service by mid-1981.

Our sincere thanks to the Boeing Vertol Company for sharing with our readers their interesting and highly successful line of helicopters for both civilian and military use. I am sure that their many contributions to rotary-wing flight in the past are just a beginning compared to what we can expect in the future.

Enstrom Helicopters

The following information, illustrations and photographs were supplied and are presented through the courtesy of the Enstrom Helicopter Corporation.

Enstrom helicopters are basically simple in concept with no hydraulics or complex mechanical features. The basic F-28, from which all succeeding models have been derived, was designed in 1960 to be a simple, low cost helicopter of conventional design and configuration. Since then, over 700 of this basic type have been produced.

Although conventional in most aspects, Enstrom helicopters are unique in three respects.

First, the Enstrom Model F-28 was the first commercially produced helicopter to utilize elastromeric bearings in the main rotor retention system. All subsequent models have retained this feature.

Secondly, the Enstrom was the first helicopter to feature aesthetic styling, proving that a helicopter could be beautifully styled and perform well. in fact, its clean aerodynamic styling accounts for it being the fastest of the light two and three-place helicopters. Its attractive styling led to its acceptance by private owners—a market that was not judged to exist to any extent, yet is now a large portion of Enstrom's business.

The Enstrom is thirdly unique in that all main rotor controls are contained within the rotor mast, a feature retained in all subsequent versions.

Model 280C Shark. The Enstrom Model 280C Shark is a three-place, turbocharged business and pleasure helicopter with unlimited operations. It is powered by a Lycoming advanced H10-360-E1AD 4-cylinder fuel injected engine rated at 205-horsepower. See Tables 4-2, 4-3 and Figs. 4-23 and 4-24.

Model F-28C-2. The Enstrom Model F-28C-2 is a function-ally designed three-place, turbocharged utility and high visibility

Table 4-2. Enstrom 280C Shark Specifications.

WEIGHT	
Empty Weight	
(basic equipped machine)*	1,500 lbs
Gross Weight	2,350 lbs
Useful Load*	850 lbs
CG Travel (indiscriminate loading)**	92" to 100"
Lycoming HIO-360-E1AD	
4-cyl engine with Rajay	
Turbocharger 301-E-10-2	205 hp
ROTOR SYSTEM	
Number of Blades, Main Rotor	3
Chord, Main Rotor Blades	9.5"
Disk Area, Main Rotor	804 sq ft
Main Rotor rpm	350
Number of Blades, Tail Rotor	2
Tail Rotor Diameter	4.78'
Chord, Tail Rotor Blade	4.4"
DIMENSIONS	
Tread—Landing Gear	7'4"
Rotor Diameter	32'
Height (overall)	9'2"
Length (overall)	29'4"
Cabin Width at Seat	61"
FUEL	
Fuel Capacity (40 gal)	240 lbs
Fuel Usable (38 gal)	228 lbs
OIL CAPACITY (10 qts)	18.7 lbs
BAGGAGE	
Volume	7 cu ft
Capacity	108 lbs

helicopter with unlimited operations. It is powered by a Lycoming H10-360-E1AD 4-cylinder fuel injected engine rated at 205-horsepower. See Tables 4-4, 4-5 and Figs. 4-25 and 4-26.

Enstrom has enjoyed a very enviable position in the helicopter market since its introduction in 1960. Their beautifully designed and appointed ships have shown prospective customers that they care about details. Their success in the future is assured with this kind of attitude. Our sincere thanks for this intimate look at their helicopters.

Table 4-3. Enstrom 280C Shark Performance.

MAXIMUM SPEED (Vne demonstrated at minimum rotor rpm)	117 mph IAS, SL to 3000 ft
CRUISING SPEEDS Vh Cruise Speed Economic Cruise Speed	110 mph 95 mph
RANGE & ENDURANCE Maximum Endurance Maximum Range (no reserve)	3.7 hrs 266 st mi
CLIMB PERFORMANCE Best Rate of Climb at SL Maximum Approved Operating Ceiling	1,150 fpm 12,000 ft
HOVER PERFORMANCE Hovering Ceiling (OGE) Hovering Ceiling (IGE) Note: Helicopter approved for restricted category operations to 2600 lbs	2,350 lbs 2,200 lbs 4,100 ft 8,300 ft 8,800 ft 13,000 ft

Hiller Aviation Company

The following information, illustrations and photographs were supplied and are presented through the courtesy of Hiller Aviation.

Hiller spans the world. In nearly 100 countries on six continents, for uses as varied as agricultural spraying, sling work, police patrol, and heavy construction, the name of Hiller has become synonymous with quality engineering and innovative research in helicopter design and manufacture. Hiller Aviation, together with Helicopter Exporters, a subsidiary of Hiller Aviation, is involved in all phases of helicopter marketing, service and production.

In late 1972, Hiller Aviation purchased all rights to Hiller helicopters from Fairchild Industries. Despite a ten-year hiatus in production of Hiller helicopters by Fairchild, President E. L. Trupe and other top officials of the company realized that a strong demand for the tried and proven UH 12s still existed.

Designed in 1946 by Stanley Hiller, the prototype UH 12 family has lived up to a basic concept through three decades of

Fig. 4-23. Enstrom 280C Shark.

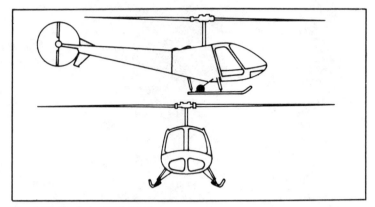

Fig. 4-24. Enstrom 280C Shark.

Table 4-4. Enstrom F-28C-2 Specifications.

WEIGHTS	
Empty Weight	
(basic equipped machine)*	1500 lbs
Gross Weight	2350 lbs
Useful Load	850 lbs
CG Travel	
(indiscriminate loading)**	92" to 100"
POWERPLANT	
Lycoming HIO-360-E1AD	
4-cyl engine with Rajay	
Turbocharger 301-E-10-2	205 hp
ROTOR SYSTEM	
Number of Blades, Main Rotor	3
Chord, Main Rotor Blades	9.5"
Disk Areas, Main Rotor	804 sq ft
Main Rotor rpm	350
Number of Blades, Tail Rotor	2
Diameter	4.78'
Chord, Tail Rotor Blade	4.4"
DIMENSIONS	
Tread—Landing Gear	7'4"
Rotor Diameter	32'
Height (overall)	9'2'
Length (overall)	27'8"
Cabin Width at Seat	59"
FUEL	
Fuel Capacity (40 gal)	240 lbs
Fuel Usable (38 gal)	228 lbs
OIL CAPACITY (10 qts)	18.7 lbs
BAGGAGE	
Volume	7 cu ft
Capacity	108 lbs

Table 4-5. Enstrom F-28C-2 Performance.

MAXIMUM SPEED (Vne demonstrated at minimum rotor rpm)	112 mph IAS, SL to 3000 ft
CRUISING SPEEDS Vh Cruise Speed Economic Cruise Speed	107 mph 85 mph
RANGE & ENDURANCE Maximum Endurance Maximum Range (no reserve)	3.7 hrs 270 st mi
CLIMB PERFORMANCE Best Rate of Climb at SL Maximum Approved Operating Ceiling	1,150 fpm 12,000 ft
HOVER PERFORMANCE Hovering Ceiling (OGE) Hovering Ceiling (IGE) NOTE: Helicopter approved for restricted category operations to 2600 lbs	2,350 lbs 2,200 lbs 4,100 ft 8,300 ft 8,800 ft 13,000 ft

demanding service in military and commercial applications. Today's UH 12E, the product of continuous research and the latest developments, is powered by a 340-horsepower Lycoming VO-540 engine, derated to 305 HP. The Soloy conversion for the UH 12E gives turbine power for the proven UH 12E helicopters.

The Research and Development department of Hiller Aviation is continually striving toward improved performance of Hiller

Fig. 4-25. Enstrom F-28C-2.

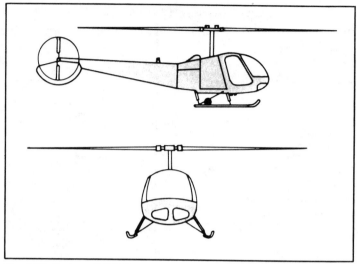

Fig. 4-26. Enstrom F-28C-2.

ships. Latest design, engineering and manufacturing techniques have dramatically reduced obsolescence, giving the UH 12E the highest ratings in the industry on main rotor blades (6670 hours) and tail rotor blades (5400 hours).

Hiller Research developed and brought about certification on the new and improved main rotor blade for the UH 12E which has reduced erosion, increased altitude and lifting capabilities, and greatly improved autorotation handling characteristics. See Figs. 4-27 through 4-31 and Tables 4-6 through 4-13.

Hiller is one of those companies where its co-founder and President, Mr. E. L. Trupe, started in the ranks. Mr. Trupe is a veteran of 26 years in aviation, 15 of which were spent in maintenance, support and production of Hiller helicopters. Hiller is in the forefront of the industry and will remain a major factor in years to come.

Our thanks to the Hiller organization for this enlightening material.

Hughes Helicopters

The following information, photographs and illustrations were supplied and are presented through the courtesy of Hughes Helicopters, Division of Summa Corporation.

Hughes Helicopters bears the name of its founder, Howard R. Hughes. Mr. Hughes was one of the pioneer fliers and builders of

Fig. 4-27. Hiller UH 12E.

special purpose aircraft during aviation's glorious golden era. During the 1930s and 1940s, Howard Hughes set and reset some of aviation's most important speed and distance records and received some of its most prestigeous awards. His contributions in the field of aircraft design and construction were no less impressive. The H1 racer and the fabulous Hughes Hercules Flying Boat, better known as the Spruce Goose, are just two (for a detailed look at the latter, see TAB Book 2320, *Howard Hughes and the Spruce Goose*).

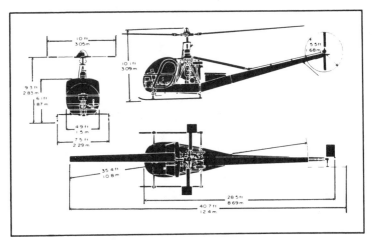

Fig. 4-28. Hiller UH 12E.

Fig. 4-29. Hiller UH 12ET.

148

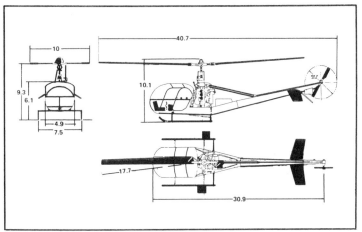

Fig. 4-30. Hiller UH 12E4.

It was only natural that he would enter the world of helicopters, which he did in the 1950s with the "Flying Crane." Today Hughes Helicopters is a leader in the industry with both civilian and military ships. In the civilian helicopter field, Hughes offers two very versatile high performance models, the 300C and the 500D.

Fig. 4-31. Hiller UH 12E4T.

Table 4-6. Hiller UH 12E Specifications.

ENGINE	Lycoming Model VO-540-C2A 6 Cylinder Opposed Air-Cooled
HORSEPOWER RATING	305 HP@3200 RPM@3000 Ft
MAIN ROTOR GEAR RATIO	8.66 to 1
ANTI-TORQUE TAIL ROTOR GEAR RATIO	1.44 to 1
NEW MAIN ROTOR BLADES	Stainless Steel (Bonded) Aluminum Honey-Comb Construction 6670 Hours Finite Life
BASIC BODY	Semi-Monocoque Construction
BLADDER TYPE FUEL CELL	46 Gallons
TAIL BOOM	Aluminum Alloy Semi-Monocoque Construction
LANDING GEAR	Mon-Retractable Skids for Easy Cabin Acess

Model 300C. For a look at this fine, low-cost maximum performance ship see Fig. 4-32.

Model 500D. For a detailed look at this fine low cost maximum performance ship see Figs. 4-33 through 4-35 and Table 4-14. Also see Appendix A, which contains a summary of the Hughes 500D flight manual.

Hughes' current production and advanced engineering activities promises a bright future for the industry as a whole, and

Table 4-7. Hiller UH 12E Performance.

MAXIMUM WEIGHT	3,100	lbs
EMPTY WEIGHT	1,759	lbs
USEFUL LOAD	1,341	lbs
MAXIMUM PERMISSABLE SPEED	96	mph
CRUISE SPEED	90	mph
RANGE AT SEA LEVEL	215	mi
ENDURANCE (No Reserve)	2.7	hrs
MAXIMUM RATE OF CLIMB	1,290	ft/min
VERTICAL RATE OF CLIMB	740	ft/min
HOVER CEILING OGE	6,800	ft
HOVER CEILING IGE	10,400	ft
MAXIMUM APPROVED ALT	15,000	ft

Hughes in particular. This company's activities, including design and development of modern, high performing versatile helicopters, are living up to the name of its Aviation Hall of Fame founder.

The Robinson R22

The following information, photographs and illustrations were supplied and are presented through the courtesy of the Robinson Helicopter Company, Inc.

Table 4-8. Hiller UH 12 ET Specifications.

ENGINE (Weight — 158 lbs)	Allison Model 250-C20B Turbine (JP4 - JP5 Fuel) Free Turbo Shaft
HORSEPOWER RATING 420 Derated to 301	301 HP@100% N2@3000 Ft
MAIN ROTOR GEAR RATIO	16.2 to 1
ANTI-TORQUE TAIL ROTOR GEAR RATIO	2.52 to 1
BASIC BODY	Semi-Monocoque Construction
BLADDER TYPE FUEL CELL	46 Gallons
TAIL BOOM	Aluminum Alloy Semi-Monocoque Construstion
LANDING GEAR	Non-Retractable Skids for Easy Cabin Access

150

Table 4-9. Hiller UH 12ET Performance.

MAXIMUM WEIGHT	3,100	lbs
EMPTY WEIGHT	1,650	lbs
USEFUL LOAD	1,450	lbs
MAXIMUM PERMISSABLE SPEED	96	mph
CRUISE SPEED	90	mph
RANGE AT SEA LEVEL	351	mi
ENDURANCE (With Aux. Tanks)	3.54 hrs	
MAXIMUM RATE OF CLIMB	1,706	ft/min
VERTICAL RATE OF CLIMB	1,464	ft/min
HOVER CEILING OGE	7,000	ft
HOVER CEILING IGE	12,000	ft
SERVICE CEILING	12,000	ft

The R22 is a low cost ultra-light two-place helicopter for general aviation (Figs. 4-36 through 4-38 and Table 4-15). Despite its low cost, the R22 is a high performance, attractive helicopter which incorporates the latest rotary-wing technology. Its large diameter rotor, low weight, and very clean fuselage combine to provide a cruise speed over 100 mph and a fuel consumption of 12 or 13 air miles per gallon.

Table 4-10. Hiller UH 12E4 Specifications.

MAXIMUM WEIGHT	3,100	lbs
EMPTY WEIGHT	1,836	lbs
USEFUL LOAD	1,264	lbs
MAXIMUM PERMISSABLE SPEED	95	mph
CRUISE SPEED	90	mph
RANGE AT SEA LEVEL	215	mi
ENDURANCE (No Reserve)	2.7 hrs	
MAXIMUM RATE OF CLIMB	993	ft/min
VERTICAL RATE OF CLIMB	740	ft/min
HOVER CEILING OGE	6,800	ft
HOVER CEILING IGE	10,400	ft
MAXIMUM APPROVED ALT	15,000	ft

To reduce the initial and operating costs, the entire design has been kept very simple, lightweight, and efficient. The control system and drive system have surprisingly few moving parts.

The unique cyclic control stick* eliminates many moving parts, while providing dual controls for training and easy entry into the helicopter. The cyclic grip moves and feels exactly the same as any other helicopter but without the undesirable stick between the

Table 4-11. Hiller UH 12E4 Performance.

ENGINE	Lycoming Model VO-540-C2A 6 Cylinder Opposed Air-Cooled
HORSEPOWER RATING	305 HP@3200 RPM 3000 Ft
MAIN ROTOR GEAR RATIO	8.66 to 1
ANTI-TORQUE TAIL ROTOR GEAR RATIO	1.44 to 1
NEW MAIN ROTOR BLADES	Stainless Steel (Bonded) Aluminum Honey-Comb Construction 6670 Hours Finite Life
BASIC BODY	Semi-Monocoque Construction
BLADDER TYPE FUEL CELL	46 Gallons
TAIL BOOM	Aluminum Alloy Semi-Monocoque Construction
LANDING GEAR	Mon-Retractable Skids for Easy Cabin Access

Table 4-12. Hiller UH 12E4T Specifications.

ENGINE (Weight — 158 lbs.)	Allison Model 250-C20B Turbine (JP4 - JP5 Fuel) Free Turbo Shaft
HORSEPOWER RATING 420 Derated to 301	301 HP@100% Nz@3000 Ft.
MAIN ROTOR GEAR RATIO	16.2 to 1
ANTI-TORQUE TAIL ROTOR GEAR RATIO	2.52 to 1
BASIC BODY	Semi-Monocoque Construction
BLADDER TYPE FUEL CELL	46 Gallons
TAIL BOOM	Aluminum Alloy Semi-Monocoque Construction
LANDING GEAR	Non-Retractable Skids for Easy Cabin Access

pilot's knees. In contrast to other two-bladed helicopters, the control forces are extremely light and there is no noticeable stick shake. This is due primarily to the unique tri-hinge rotor head. The handling characteristics were also improved by phasing the main rotor controls to reduce undesirable control coupling, and by providing high-lift cambered tail rotor blades for positive yaw control.

Ground handling and storage of the R22 is simplified by its low weight and two-bladed rotor. It is easily maneuvered on ground handling wheels by one man and can be stored in a hangar area only about one-third of that required for a light airplane or multi-bladed helicopter.

Another feature is the teeter-hinge restraint* which helps keep the rotor level during starting and stopping. This reduces the dangerous see-saw teetering motion typical of many two-bladed helicopters. The restraint is only active at low RPM and does not interfere with the free teetering of the rotor during flight. This feature, combined with a rotor height over eight feet, improves head clearance under the rotating blades.

Robinson is a new name on the horizon and much is promised and expected from this company in the future. Their R22 has stirred great interest by all who have seen and flown her.

Table 4-13. Hiller UH 12E4T Performance.

MAXIMUM WEIGHT	3,100	lbs
EMPTY WEIGHT	1,650	lbs
USEFUL LOAD	1,450	lbs
MAXIMUM PERMISSIBLE SPEED	96	mph
CRUISE SPEED	90	mph
RANGE AT SEA LEVEL	351	mi
ENDURANCE (With Aux. Tanks)	3.54	hrs
MAXIMUM RATE OF CLIMB	1,706	ft/min
VERTICAL RATE OF CLIMB	1,463	ft/min
HOVER CEILING OGE	7,000	ft
HOVER CEILING IGE	12,000	ft
SERVICE CEILING	12,000	ft

Fig. 4-32. Hughes 300C.

153

Fig. 4-33. Hughes 500D.

154

Fig. 4-34. Hughes 500C.

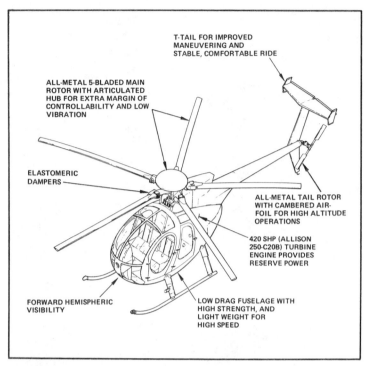

Fig. 4-35. Hughes 500D operating features.

Fig. 4-36. Robinson R22.

Table 4-14. Hughes 500D Performance.

ITEM	2200 lb	2550 lb	3000 lb
Maximum cruise speed*, SL, TAS	168 mph	165 mph	160 mph
Maximum cruise speed, 5,000 ft, TAS	168 mph	165 mph	155 mph
Economic cruise speed, SL, TAS	145 mph	145 mph	150 mph
Economic cruise speed, 5,000 ft, TAS	145 mph	145 mph	145 mph
Hover ceiling OGE**, takeoff power			
Standard Atmosphere (ISA)	16,500 ft	12,500 ft	7,500 ft
ISA plus 20°C	14,000 ft	10,000 ft	4,500 ft
35°C (95°F)***	6,000 ft	6,000 ft	4,500 ft
Hover ceiling IGE**, 3-foot skid height, takeoff power			
Standard atmosphere (ISA)	17,000 ft	13,000 ft	8,500 ft
ISA plus 20°C	15,000 ft	10,500 ft	6,000 ft
35°C (95°F)***	6,000 ft	6,000 ft	4,500 ft
Maximum rate of climb at sea level, takeoff power			
Standard atmosphere (ISA)	3,000 fpm	2,500 fpm	1,900 fpm
ISA plus 20°C	3,000 fpm	2,500 fpm	1,900 fpm
Vertical rate of climb at sea level, takeoff power	2,500 fpm	1,900 fpm	900 fpm
Service ceiling (100 fpm at maximum continuous power)	20,000 ft	20,000 ft	15,000 ft
Range, 2-minute warmup, no reserves, standard atmosphere (ISA)			
Sea level	320 mi	320 mi	300 mi
5,000 ft	370 mi	355 mi	330 mi
Endurance, 2-minute warmup, no reserves, standard atmosphere (ISA)			
Sea level	3.2 hr	3.0 hr	2.8 hr
5,000 ft	3.6 hr	3.4 hr	3.1 hr

*Maximum speed, V_{ne}, sea level, for all weights in 175 mph
**Performance for Hughes 500D is attainable in sidewinds of up to 23 mph
***Limited by engine operating and starting limits

NOTE: The above performance is based on the Allison Model Specification C847-B for 250-C20B engine and applies under the following conditions: standard atmosphere unless noted, clean flight configuration, a 30-ampere, 28-volt generator load, engine anti-icing off, 103% N_2, and engine limits of 87.9 psi torque takeoff (375 hp) and 82 psi torque maximum continuous operation (350 hp)

Fig. 4-37. Robinson R22.

Table 4-15. Robinson R22 Weights and Performance.

Weights

Gross Weight ....1300 lb
Empty Weight (with full oil)...796 lb
Fuel (20 gal) ....120 lb
Pilot, Passenger & Optional Equipment ....384 lb

Performance

Maximum Airspeed (VNE) ....118 MPH
Cruise Airspeed @ 75% Power ....108 MPH
Approx Range (No Reserve)..240 Miles
Fuel Consumption ....12 Miles/Gal
Rate-of-Climb at S L ....1200 FPM
Rate-of-Climb at 5000 feet..1060 FPM
Service Ceiling ....14,000 Feet
Hover Ceiling IGE ....6,500 Feet
Hover Ceiling OGE ....4,500 Feet

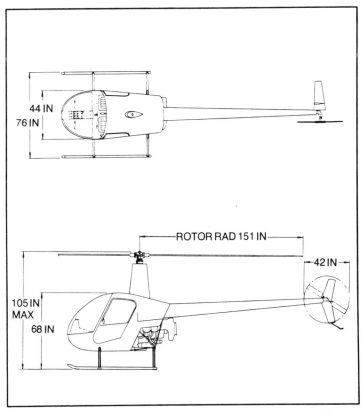

Fig. 4-38. Robinson R22, general arrangement.

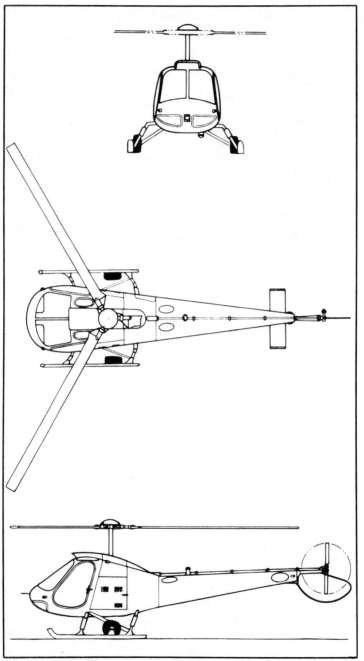

Fig. 4-39. Spitfire Mark I.

Fig. 4-40. Spitfire Mark I controls.

161

Fig. 4-41. Spitfire Mark II.

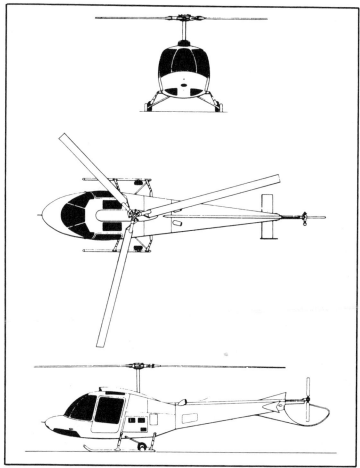

Fig. 4-42. Spitfire Mark II general arrangement.

Table 4-16. Spitfire Mark I Specifications.

Max Gross Weight ....2350 lbs	Max Cont SHP ....420 SHP Derated
Empty Weight ....1250 lbs	Max Airspeed Vne ....129 mph
Useful Load ....1100 lbs	Cruise ....110 mph
w/Full Fuel ....645 lbs	Max Rate of Climb ....1550 fpm
Max external load ....1100 lbs	Fuel Capacity ....70 gal
Seating 3	Fuel Consumption ....25 gph
Baggage Comp ....20 cu ft	Max Range ....308 sm
Rotor Diameter ....32.0 ft	Max Endurance ....4 hrs
Overall Length ....32.0 ft	Hover IGE ....13,400 ft
Overall Height ....9.2 ft	Hover OGE ....8,000 ft
Fuselage Length ....29.4 ft	Service Ceiling ....15,000 ft
Rotor Blades 3	
Type ....fully articulated	
Powerplant ....Allison 250 .C20 B	

Fig. 4-43. Spitfire Taurus.

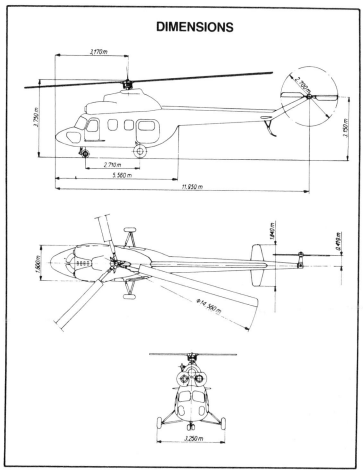

Fig. 4-44. Spitfire Taurus, general arrangement.

Table 4-17. Spitfire Mark II Specifications.

Max Gross Weight	2500 lbs	Max Cont SHP	420 SHP Derated
Empty Weight	1325 lbs	Max Airspeed Vne	135 mph
Useful Load	1175 lbs	Cruise	120 mph
w/Full Fuel	720 lbs	Max Rate of Climb	1550 fpm
Max external load	1400 lbs	Fuel Capacity	70 gal
Seating	4	Fuel Consumption	25 gph
Baggage Comp	20 cu ft	Max Range	308 sm
Rotor Diameter	32.0 ft	Max Endurance	4 hrs
Overall Length	32.0 ft	Hover IGE	13,400 ft
Overall Height	9.2 ft	Hover OGE	8,000 ft
Fuselage Length	30.5 ft	Service Ceiling	15,000 ft
Rotor Blades	3		
Type	fully articulated		
Powerplant	Allison 250-C20 B		

165

Table 4-18. Spitfire Taurus General Characteristics.

Arrangement:

Passenger-transport:	1 pilot + 8 passengers in standard version
	1 pilot + 6 passengers in executive version
Casualty evacuation:	1 pilot + 3 stretchers—patients + 1 place
	for seated patient or doctor
Cargo carrying:	1 pilot + 5, 6 m³ (197.76 cu. ft.) load in cabin or
	1 pilot + 1000 kg (2,202.6 lb.) on cargo sling

Weights:-

	kg	lb
Empty weight, standard aircraft		
Engine oil	2140.00	4718.00
Useful load	10.00	22.00
Max. weight on take-off	1400.00	3086.00
	3550.00	7826.00

Power-plant:

2 Allison 250C-20B turbine engines
Power-ratings in standard atmosphere, at sea level (for 1 engine)

Take-off (5 min)	420 HP
30-Minute Power	420 HP
Max. Cont	400 HP
Max. Cruise	370 HP
Cruise A (90%)	333 HP
Cruise A (75%)	278 HP

Fuel capacity (usable fuel):

Standard tank 600 litres 158.5 US gal. 462 kg 1,017 lb
Additional tanks (option) 480 litres 126.82 US gal. 370 kg 815 lb

Certification:

Polish and in 1980 U.S.A. in accordance with FAR 29, category A, for day and night VFR flying.
IFR approval pending.

Table 4-19. Spitfire Taurus Performance.

			Normal T.O. weight	Max. T.O. weight
Take-off weight	kg	3,150	3,350	3,550
	lb	6,946	7,386	7,827
VNE	km/hr	250	250	250
	mph	155	155	155
	kts	135	135	135
Fast cruise speed	km/hr	225	220	210
	mph	139	137	130
	kts	121	119	113
Economical cruise speed	km/hr	190	190	190
	mph	121	121	120
	kts	105	105	105
Fuel consumption at	kg/km	0.87	0.91	0.96
economical cruise speed	lb/st.m	3.08	3.23	3.41
	lb/n.m	3.56	3.72	3.92
Rate of climb	m/sec	8.4	7.5	6.7
	ft/min	1,653	1,476	1,319
Rate of climb one engine	m/sec	1.6	1.1	0.7
Operates (max. cont. power)	ft/min.	315	216	138
Max. range without fuel	km	522	510	497
Reserve at economical	st. m	324	317	309
cruise speed, std. tank	n. m	282	275	268
Max. endurance				
Without reserve, std. tank	hr	3.41	3.27	3.15
Hover ceiling IGE at	m	2,560	1,940	1,320
Take-off power	ft	8,399	6,365	4,331
Hover ceiling OGE at	m	1,860	1,240	480
Take-off power	ft	6,102	4,068	1,575
Service ceiling	m	>4,000	>4,000	4,000
(0.5 m/s—100 ft/min.)	ft	>13,123	>13,123	13,123

Operating limitations
The aircraft is cleared to operate within the following altitude and temperature limitations:
—Maximum pressure altitude—4,000 m—13,123 ft
—Maximum temperature + 40°C
—Minimum temperature—40°C
PROVISIONALLY, the max. gross weight is limited to 3,550 kg (7,827 lb)

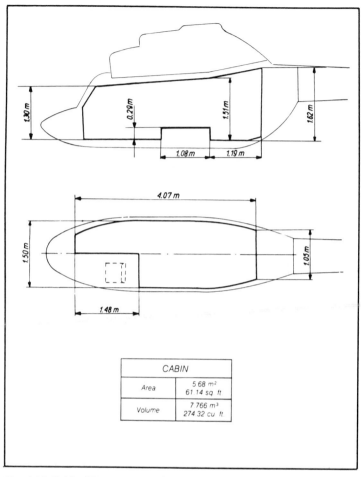

CABIN	
Area	5.68 m² 61.14 sq. ft.
Volume	7.766 m³ 274.32 cu. ft.

Fig. 4-45. Spitfire Taurus, interior dimensions.

Spitfire Helicopter Company, Ltd.

The following information, photographs and illustrations were supplied and are presented through the courtesy of the Spitfire Helicopter Company, Ltd.

The Spitfire Helicopter Company, Ltd. of Pennsylvania markets the Spitfire Mark I and Mark II Taurus line of helicopters. They are manufactured by Swidnik in Poland. A closer look at these ships will reveal some interesting design features. See Figs. 4-39 through 4-45 and Tables 4-16 through 4-19.

Appendix A

The Hughes 500 Flight Manual

Editor's Note: The following information is presented for the reader's familiarity *only*, and should serve to illustrate the procedures and systems involved in a modern helicopter. *Always* obtain and use the manufacturer's own flight manual for the particular helicopter that you wish to operate.

GENERAL

Introduction

The *Pilot's Flight Manual* has been prepared with but one very fundamental goal in mind: to provide the pilot with all information necessary to accomplish the intended mission with the maximum amount of safety and economy possible.

General. Information of general interest to the pilot, owner, or operator of the aircraft.

Limitations. Specifically defines the limiting factors, procedures, and regime within which the aircraft may be operated.

Emergency and Malfunction Procedures. Each type of problem normally encountered in flight is defined, and the procedures necessary to cope with or alleviate the situation are given. The data is recommended by the manufacturer as appropriate.

Normal Procedures. Normal operation from engine start onward. As with emergency procedures, the data given is that recommended by the manufacturer as appropriate.

Performance Data. Aircraft performance is defined within certain conditions; some of these are airspeed, weight, altitude, temperature, humidity, and wind velocity. The data given is in tabular or graph form and allows the pilot to determine his aircraft's capabilities related to the intended mission and the conditions which are current.

Weight and Balance Data. Aircraft weight and balance are major operational factors. Data is provided by chart, graph, and examples which allow the pilot to accurately determine the aircraft's gross weight and whether the load is distributed within the fore and aft, and lateral center of gravity limits.

Aircraft Handling, Servicing, and Maintenance. The information contained in this section is extracted from the *Handbook of Maintenance Instructions* and is highly selective. The subjects chosen are those with which the pilot will have direct involvement, either while at his normal base of operations or in the field.

Additional Operations and Performance Data. The section on Performance Data provides all basic data required and approved by the FAA. The information in the section on Additional Operations and Performance Data is given by the manufacturer to further inform the pilot of the aircraft's capabilities and allow him, by the use of graphs and tables, to utilize his aircraft to a maximum degree.

Optional Equipment Supplements. A number of pieces of optional equipment are available for the performance of specific tasks. In many cases, the equipment is readily removable and may be used in combination(s) with other optional items whenever the installation of an option affects Limitations, Procedures, or Performance.

Method of Presentation. General information in the various sections is presented in narrative form. Other information is given in step-by-step procedures, graphs, charts, or tabular form.

The information in the step-by-step procedure is presented in the imperative mode; each statement describes a particular operation to be accomplished. Expansion of the steps is accomplished as follows:

Note

Notes are used to expand and explain the preceding step and provide fuller understanding of the reason for the particular operation.

Caution

Cautions are used to alert the individual that damage to equipment may result if the procedural step is not followed to the letter.

Warning

Warnings are used to bring to the pilot's immediate attention that not only damage to equipment but personal injury may occur if the instruction is disregarded.

Helicopter Description

The Hughes 500D is a fast lightweight, turbine-powered, all-purpose helicopter (Fig. A-1).

The 500D has been designed so as to allow rapid configuration changes. Thus, the aircraft may be converted from a personnel transport to a utility cargo or maximum density personnel carrier. Typical uses include the following:

☐ Key Personnel transport (up to 5);
☐ High density personnel transport (up to 7);
☐ Ambulance configuration;
☐ Internal, external cargo capability;
☐ Aerial survey, patrol, and photographic missions;
☐ Air-sea rescue - amphibious capability;
☐ Agricultural capabilities;
☐ Forestry, fire fighting, and police application.

Note

Certification of the Model 369D Helicopter was performed at a maximum continuous power setting of 779°C, and the helicopter is fully capable of operating continuously at that power setting. The engine manufacturer, however, specifies that if the engine is operated continuously up to 74.3-psi torque (320 shp), the maximum TOT is 755°C. For continuous power in excess of 74.3-psi torque, but not exceeding 81.3-psi torque, the maximum TOT is 738°C. If the engine is operated in excess of these values, the engine warranty will not be honored. Therefore, the TOT indicator is marked with a yellow arc from 755°C to 810°C; and a blue dot at 738°C; and the torque indicator is marked with a blue dot at 74.3-psi torque.

Design and Construction Description

The Hughes 500D helicopter is a turbine-powered, rotary-wing aircraft constructed primarily of aluminum alloy. The main

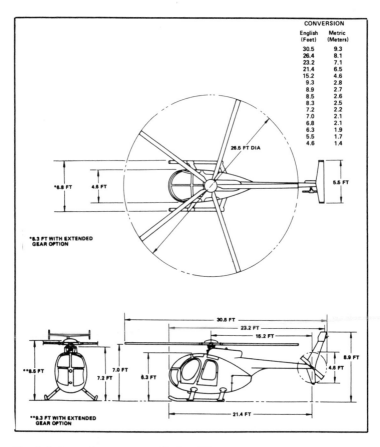

CONVERSION	
English (Feet)	Metric (Meters)
30.5	9.3
26.4	8.1
23.2	7.1
21.4	6.5
15.2	4.6
9.3	2.8
8.9	2.7
8.5	2.6
8.3	2.5
7.2	2.2
7.0	2.1
6.8	2.1
6.3	1.9
5.5	1.7
4.6	1.4

Fig. A-1. General arrangement, Hughes 500.

rotor is five-bladed and fully articulated; the tail rotor is a two-bladed, antitorque semi-rigid-type. Power from the turboshaft engine is coupled to the main and tail rotors by drive shafts and two transmissions. An overruning (one-way) clutch in the drive between the engine and main transmission permits free-wheeling of the rotors for autorotational descent.

The fuselage (with a central framework consisting of a mast-support structure, two bulkheads, and center beam) is a semi-monocoque structure that is divided into three main sections. The forward section comprises a pilot compartment and directly aft a cargo and/or passenger compartment separated by a bulkhead. The pilot compartment is equipped with seat for the pilot and either one or two passengers. A canopy of transparent, tinted acrylic

171

panels provides excellent visibility. The left seat in the pilot's compartment (looking forward) is the pilot's seat (command position); in special military-version helicopters, the pilot's seat is on the right side.

The standard 500D requires a minimum crew of one pilot seated in the left side of the compartment. The passengers sit to the right and abreast of the pilot, one positioned at the aircraft centerline and the other on the far right; seat belts are provided for all positions. In the special military version, the center seat is eliminated.

An instrument panel is located forward of the seats at the aircraft centerline. The panel incorporates standard flight and engine instruments in addition to warning and caution lights. The panel also contains adequate space provisions for various arrangements of communication and navigation equipment.

The lower fuselage structure beneath the pilot/passenger floor contains compartment space for the aircraft battery and provision for small-cargo storage or installation of avionics equipment. Access to the compartments is through two floor doorplates.

The cargo compartment in the center of the aircraft, behind the pilot compartment, contains provisions for installation of two bench- or folding-type passenger seats.

Seat belts are provided and several styles are offered. The seats and belts are readily removable. High density operations may be conducted with up to four persons utilizing an optional seat and belt kit. Cargo compartment bench-type seats may be easily folded out of the way or completely removed for accommodation of cargo.

During cargo-carrying operations, the compartment floor serves as the cargo deck. Readily removable and interchangeable cargo tiedown fittings are available.

The aft section includes the structure for the tailboom attachment and the engine-mounts and engine. Access to the engine compartment is provided through clamshell doors contoured to the shape of the fuselage.

The lower section is divided by the center beam and provides a housing for the two fuel cells. Provisions for the attachment of a cargo hook are located on the bottom of the fuselage in line with the center beam.

The power plant used is the Allison Model 250-C20B gas-turbine engine with a takeoff power rating of 420 shp. Only 375 shp at 103 percent rpm is used for takeoff; 350 maximum continuous shp provides sufficient power for all other flight modes.

Use of less than maximum available power provides a higher engine critical altitude. The power turbine governor provides automatic constant speed control of rotor rpm.

The overrunning clutch transmits power from the engine to the main drive shaft. The clutch needs no external controls and disengages automatically during autorotation and engine shutdown. The main shaft connects to the transmission input shaft. The engine oil cooler blower is belt driven off the main drive shaft. The oil cooler blower draws cooling air from the engine inlet, in addition to supplying ambient air to the engine oil cooler, transmission oil cooler, and engine compartment area.

The main transmission is mounted on the basic airframe structure above the passenger/cargo compartment. The transmission has a separate lubrication and oil supply system; cooling is by use of a separate oil cooler.

The main rotor static mast is nonrotating and is rigidly attached to the basic airframe structure. The rotor hub is supported by the rotor mast.

Torque is transmitted independently to the rotor through the main rotor drive shaft, thus lifting loads are prevented from being imposed onto the main transmission with resultant thrust loading of transmission parts.

Four doors are installed on the helicopter, two on each side of the fuselage, for entry and degrees of personnel and cargo. The two forward doors permit access to the forward compartment for pilot and passengers. The two aft doors permit access to the aft passenger/cargo compartment. Transparent tinted windows are contained in the doors.

The tailboom is a monocoque structure of aluminum alloy frames and skin. The tailboom is the supporting attachment structure for the stabilizers, tail rotor transmission, and tail rotor.

The tailboom also houses the tail rotor transmission drive shaft; the one-piece dynamically balanced shaft requires no intermediate couplings or bearings. Metallic diaphragm shaft-end-couplings are used.

The tail rotor transmission is mounted on the aft end of the tailboom and has a self-contained lubricant system. The tail rotor is mounted on the output shaft of the transmission and consists of two variable-pitch blades.

The main rotor group consists of the five main rotor blades, a fully articulated main rotor hub assembly with offset flapping hinges, a scissors assembly, and a swashplate and associated mixer control mechanisms. The main rotor blades are secured to the rotor hub assembly with standard hardware and quick-release lever-type pins.

The pilot's cyclic control stick (Fig. A-2) and adjustable tail rotor control pedals are directly in front of the pilot's seat. The collective pitch control stick is located on the left of the pilot's seat. The entire control system is a solid, mechanically linked type, using tubular push-pull rods. The copilot's (dual control installation) is similar but is readily removable from the aircraft.

The nonretractable landing gear is a horizontal, skid-type gear, attached to the fuselage at 12 points. Aerodynamic fairings cover the struts, from the fuselage to the skids. Nitrogen-charged landing gear dampers, between the struts and structure, act as shock absorbers to cushion landings and provide ground stability. Provisions for ground-handling wheels are incorporated on the skid tubes.

General Dimensional Data

This summary covers pertinent information on areas, dimensions, and airfoil data.

Rotor Characteristics	Main	Tail
Number of Blades	5	2
Rotor Diameter, feet	26.41	4.58
Rotor Disc Area, square feet	547.81	16.50
Blade Chord (constant), feet	0.562	0.442
Blade Twist, degrees	9 washout	8.6 washout
Blade Area (total blades x C x R), square feet	37.13	2.03
Solidity (thrust weighted)	0.068	0.119
Airfoil Section, NACA	0015	63-415
δ_3, degrees	0	30
Droop Stop Flapping, degrees	-6	10 soft, 15 hard
Droop Stop Coning, degrees	0 static -2 rotating	—
Built-in Collective Pitch at ¾ R (straps untwisted), degrees	8	—
Flap Hinge Offset, inches	6	—

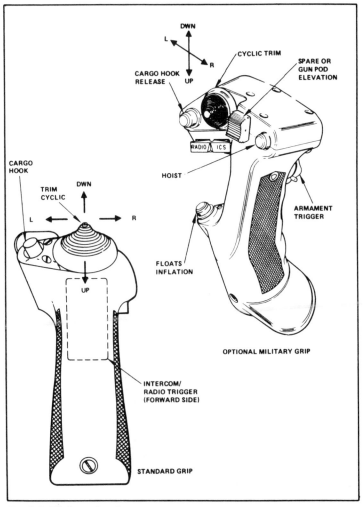

Fig. A-2. Pilot's cyclic grip.

Rotor Speeds	Engine N$_p$%	Main		Tail	
		RPM	Tip Speed ft/sec	RPM	Tip Speed ft/sec
Design Maximum-Power Off		549	759	3275	786
Maximum Redline-Power Off		523	723	3120	749
Minimum Redline-Power Off		410	567	2446	586
Design Minimum-Power Off		380	525	2266	543
Maximum-Power On	103	492	680	2933	704
Minimum-Power On	102	487	673	2904	697

T-Tail

Horizontal Stabilizer:

Span	5.33 feet
Tip Chord	1.05 feet
Root Chord	1.73 feet
Area	7.36 square feet
Airfoil Root	NACA 6518 Inverted
Airfoil Tip	NACA 6515 Inverted
Incidence	+5.0 degrees

End Plates on Horizontal Stabilizer	(2) five-sided polygons
Total Area	1.42 square feet

Upper Vertical Stabilizer - Portion above Centerline of Boom:

Span	3.54 feet
Tip Chord	0.94 foot
Root chord	1.27 feet
Area	3.91 square feet
Airfoil Root	13.4 percent thick - modified section*
Airfoil Tip	18.3 percent thick - modified section*

Lower Vertical Stabilizer - Portion below Centerline of Boom:

Span	2.29 feet
Tip Chord	0.59 foot
Root chord	1.27 feet
Area	2.14 square feet
Airfoil Root	13.4 percent thick - modified section*
Airfoil Tip	28.0 percent thick - modified section*

*Vertical stabilizer is flat sided, constant thickness (2.06 inch) section.

Control Rigging
Main Rotor

Collective Pitch, Full Travel, minimum	14.25 degrees (up to down) 0.75 R
Collective Pitch at Down Stop	0 to 3 degrees (ground adjustable)

Range of Cyclic Pitch Blade Angles from Neutral Rigging Position, minimum		
	Forward	17 degrees
	Aft	7 degrees
	Left	7 degrees
	Right	5.5 degrees

Tail Rotor

Range of Blade Pitch Angles (¾ Radius), minimum		
	Right Pedal (thrust to left)	13 degrees
	Left Pedal (thrust to right)	27 degrees

Engine.

250-C20B Engine	100 percent N_1 = 50,970 rpm/60 = 849 rps

LIMITATIONS

Rotorcraft Certification

Certification is based on an Engine Failure Warning System (including both visual and audio indications), Low Rotor RPM Warning System, and Outside Air Temperature Gauge, and Fuel Low caution light being installed and operable.

Flight Limitations

Instrument flight is prohibited.

Flight during icing conditions is prohibited.

Maximum operating altitude is 16,000 feet density altitude.

Solo flight is prohibited from the right seat (standard helicopter).

Solo flight is prohibited from the left seat (military version).

Maximum wind when hovering downwind with a cyclic trim failure (full forward) is 15 knots.

V_{NE} limited to 130 knots IAS with less than 35 pounds of fuel for all flight operations.

Further flight is prohibited until the battery has been inspected, following a battery overtemperature of 160°F and above.

Flight Restrictions

Flight operation is permitted in falling and/or blowing snow when the Automatic Engine Reignition Kit and engine failure warning system are installed and operable.

When the helicopter has been outside during falling snow, determine that the engine inlet and surrounding skin areas are completely free of accumulated ice and snow prior to the next flight.

Flight operation is permitted at night when landing, navigation, instrument, and anticollision lights are installed and operable.

Caution

"Strobe" anticollision lights should be turned off during prolonged hover or ground operation over concrete to avoid possible pilot distraction. The lights should also be turned off when entering clouds, fog, or haze to preclude optical illusions or spatial disorientation.

Flight operation at night is limited to VFR conditions.

Orientation shall be maintained through visual reference to ground objects, solely as a result of ground lights or adequate celestial illumination.

Doors-off flight operation may be conducted in accordance with the following: all doors off; both rear doors off; any one door off.

Maximum V_{NE} is 130 knots IAS for gross weights of 2501 pounds or more and 120 knots IAS for 2500 pounds or less. Variations of V_{NE} with altitude is the same as with all doors on.

Upon completion of the flight in progress, flight is prohibited until the fuel filter has been serviced when the fuel filter light has illuminated.

Flight with the center seat occupied may be conducted in accordance with the following: dual controls removed; right hand seat cushion relocated outboard and secured; center location seat back and seat cushion installed and secured; seat belt installed and operable (shoulder harness optional).

Airspeed Limits

V_{NE} is limited to 156 knots IAS.

V_{NE} is limited to 131 knots IAS during autorotation.

V_{NE} is limited to 130 knots IAS with less than 35 pounds of fuel.

V_{NE} is limited to 130 knots IAS (2501 pounds or more) and 120 knots IAS (2500 pounds or less) during doors off flight.

Rotor Speed Limits

Maximum rpm: Power off 523, power on 492 rpm (103 percent N_2).

Minimum rpm: Power off 410, power on 487 rpm (102 percent N_2).

Weight Limitations

Maximum gross weight is 3000 pounds.

Minimum front seat weight; at least two occupants are to be loaded in the front seats prior to loading rear seats or ballast, as required, must be carried.

Note

Ballast may be carried in the utility stowage compartment or stowed and secured by the seat belt and shoulder harness in the opposite front seat. Ballast may consist of shot or sandbags, or similar material adequately contained and secured.

Maximum weight in the utility stowage compartment is 50 pounds.

This helicopter is limited to operation in accordance with the approved loading information; refer to section on Weight and Balance Data.

Center of Gravity (CG Envelope)

The Datum line is 100.0 inches forward of the main rotor hub centerline.

The forward CG limit is 99.0 inches; the aft CG varies linearly from 103.0 inches at 3000 pounds gross weight, to 107.4 inches at minimum flying weight of 1538 pounds.

Lateral "+" CG is right of the aircraft centerline; lateral "−" CG is left of the centerline when looking forward (Fig. A-3).

Lateral CG is ±3 inches.

Power Plant Limits - Allison Model 250-C20B

Takeoff power (5-minute limit); 87.2-psi torque, 810°C maximum TOT.

Maximum continuous operation; 81.3-psi torque, 738°C maximum TOT.

Note

The engine is certified for maximum continuous operation at 779°C TOT. However, for warranty purposes, the engine manufacturer requires that:

1. All power settings up to 74.3-psi torque (blue dot on torquemeter) maximum TOT is 755°C.

2. All power settings between 74.3-psi torque and 81.3-psi torque maximum TOT is 738°C (blue dot on TOT indicator).

N_1 idle speed; 64 to 65 percent.

Maximum allowable output shaft speeds; overspeed limit 15 seconds 109 percent N_2 at idle power, varying linearly to 105 percent at 87.2-psi torque.

Maximum N_2 overspeed 113 percent, not to exceed 15 seconds.

TOT limits: during start and shutdown - 810° to 927°C for 10 seconds; during power changes in flight - 810° to 843°C for 6 seconds.

Minimum engine oil temperature: for takeoff is 0°C, providing engine oil pressure is within specified limits.

Note

0°C is not marked on the instrument. 0°C is when needled is at bottom of yellow arc.

Continuous operation must be accomplished between 54°C and 107°C.

Minimum engine oil pressure: 115 psi at 94.5 percent N_1 and above; 90 psi at 78.5 percent N_1; below 78.5 percent N_1, 50 psi.

Transient over torque limits: 15 seconds at 91.2-psi torque, 105 percent N_2; 3 seconds at 95.8-psi torque, 105 percent N_2.

At sea level, the maximum engine air inlet ambient temperature is 130°F varying on a straight-line basis to 6000 feet pressure

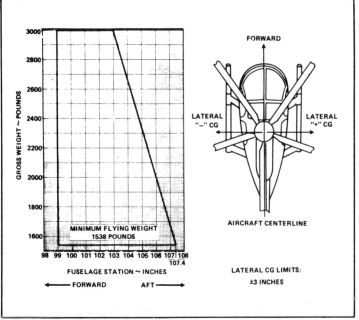

Fig. A-3. Center of gravity envelope.

altitude at a maximum temperature of 95°F varying on a straight-line basis to 20,000 feet pressure altitude at a temperature of 32°F. It is to be assumed that engine air inlet temperature is the same as ambient temperature (free air temperature) (see Figs. A-4 through A-8).

EMERGENCY AND MALFUNCTION PROCEDURES
Engine Failure

A change in noise level and a left yaw may be the first indications of an engine failure.

Blinking red light on instrument panel.

Pulsating sound from warning horn and in headset if installed.

The failure indicators are actuated when N_1 falls below 55 percent. Operation of the system may be checked when the engine is inoperative with the battery and generator switch ON. A proper air start may be attempted at the pilot's discretion.

Allow speed to reduce to the lesser of 131 knots IAS or lower. Maintain rotor speed between 410 and 523 rpm by use of collective control.

Proceed with autorotational descent and landing.

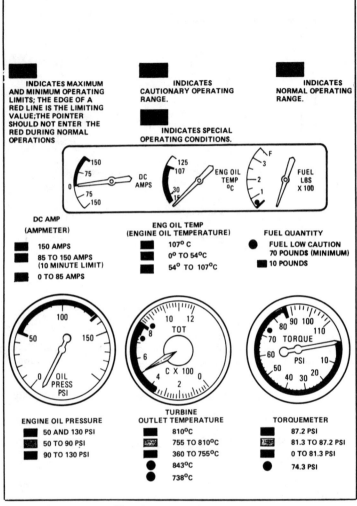

Fig. A-4. Instrument markings I.

Engine Failure - Cruising at Altitudes 500 feet and Above

Enter normal autorotation by lowering collective pitch.

Note

If airspeed is above maximum autorotational V_{NE} (131 knots), aft cyclic will be required to maintain ship's attitude and to decrease airspeed to autorotational V_{NE} as collective is lowered. Collective pitch may have to be adjusted upward after establishing autorotation to prevent rotor overspeed if the flight is being conducted at maximum gross weight or at a high density altitude. To reduce sink rate or to extend gliding distance, operate at minimum rpm; restore rotor rpm by lowering collective prior to flareout.

Select landing spot and maneuver as required.

Maximum gliding distance is obtained at 80 knots/410 rotor rpm.

Minimum rate of descent is obtained at 60 knots/410 rotor rpm.

A restart may be attempted at the discretion of the pilot.

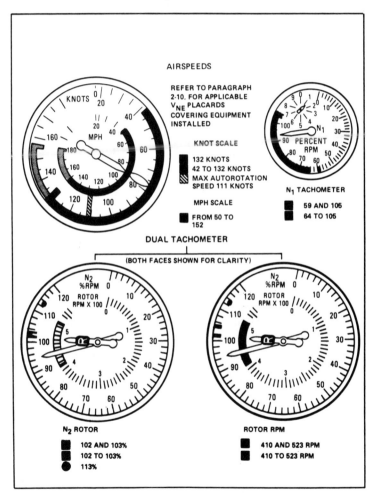

Fig. A-5. Instrument markings II.

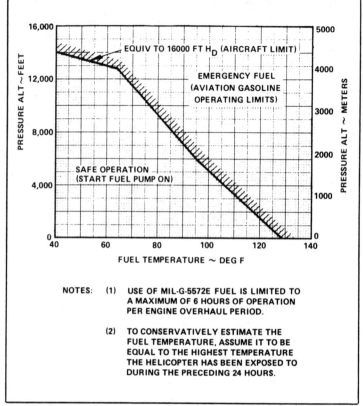

Fig. A-6. Operating limitations when using MIL-G-5572E emergency fuel (aviation gasoline).

If unable to restart, turn off unnecessary switches and cut off fuel.

Flare as required for the terrain and land in a level attitude.

Touch down in a level attitude.

Avoid the use of aft cyclic stick or rapid lowering of the collective pitch during initial ground contact or during ground slide.

In the event of engine failure at night, do not turn on landing light at more than 1000 feet above terrain; this preserves battery power.

Engine Failure - Altitude Above 12 and Below 500 Feet

Takeoff operation should be conducted in accordance with the Height Velocity Diagram (Fig. A-9).

In the event of power failure during takeoff, the collective pitch must be initially lowered in order that the rotor speed may be maintained.

The amount and duration of collective reduction depends upon the height above the ground at which the engine failure occurs.

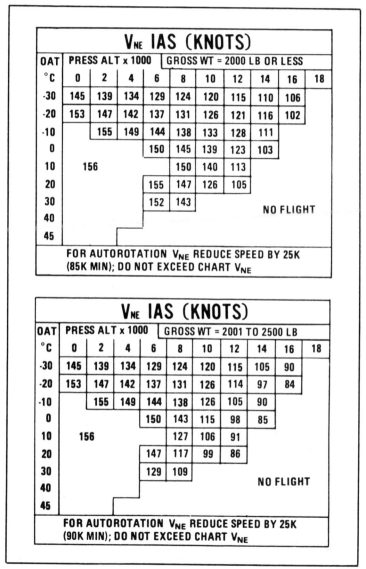

V_{NE} IAS (KNOTS)

V_{NE} IAS (KNOTS)

OAT	PRESS ALT x 1000				GROSS WT = 2000 LB OR LESS					
°C	0	2	4	6	8	10	12	14	16	18
-30	145	139	134	129	124	120	115	110	106	
-20	153	147	142	137	131	126	121	116	102	
-10		155	149	144	138	133	128	111		
0				150	145	139	123	103		
10	156				150	140	113			
20				155	147	126	105			
30				152	143			NO FLIGHT		
40										
45										

FOR AUTOROTATION V_{NE} REDUCE SPEED BY 25K (85K MIN); DO NOT EXCEED CHART V_{NE}

V_{NE} IAS (KNOTS)

OAT	PRESS ALT x 1000				GROSS WT = 2001 TO 2500 LB					
°C	0	2	4	6	8	10	12	14	16	18
-30	145	139	134	129	124	120	115	105	90	
-20	153	147	142	137	131	126	114	97	84	
-10		155	149	144	138	126	105	90		
0				150	143	115	98	85		
10	156				127	106	91			
20				147	117	99	86			
30				129	109			NO FLIGHT		
40										
45										

FOR AUTOROTATION V_{NE} REDUCE SPEED BY 25K (90K MIN); DO NOT EXCEED CHART V_{NE}

Fig. A-7. Limitations placards I.

185

OAT	PRESS ALT x 1000					GROSS WT = 2501 TO 3000 LB				
°C	0	2	4	6	8	10	12	14	16	18
-30	145	139	134	129	124	117	100	85	72	
-20	153	147	142	137	128	108	93	79	67	
-10		155	149	144	117	100	85	73		
0			128	108	93	79	68			
10	156		145	117	101	86	73			
20			130	109	94	81	69			
30		148	119	103	88		NO FLIGHT			
40		132	111							
45		127								

V_{NE} IAS (KNOTS)

FOR AUTOROTATION V_{NE} REDUCE SPEED BY 25K (95K MIN); DO NOT EXCEED CHART V_{NE}

	MINIMUM N_1 SPEED STARTING RECOMMENDATIONS		
OAT °C	-18 AND BELOW	-18 TO 7	7 AND ABOVE
N_1%	12	13	15

THIS HELICOPTER MUST BE OPERATED IN COMPLIANCE WITH THE OPERATING LIMITATIONS SPECIFIED IN THE APPROVED ROTORCRAFT FLIGHT MANUAL.

V_{NE} 130 KNOTS IAS WITH LESS THAN 35 POUNDS OF FUEL.

50 POUNDS MAXIMUM LOAD LIMIT UNIFORMLY DISTRIBUTED.

NOTE

THE PLACARD IS LOCATED INSIDE UTILITY STOWAGE COMPARTMENT.

Fig. A-8. Limitations placards II.

As the ground is approached, aft cyclic and collective controls should be used as needed to decrease forward and vertical velocity.

Ground contact should be established in a level attitude.

Engine Failure - Altitude Below 12 Feet

A power failure is indicated by a yawing of the ship to the left and loss of rotor rpm.

Do not reduce collective pitch.

Apply right pedal to prevent yawing.

Apply collective pitch as necessary in order to cushion landing.

Ditching - Power Off

Turn off battery switch.

Make autorotative approach and landing.

Level helicopter and apply full collective pitch as contact is made with water.

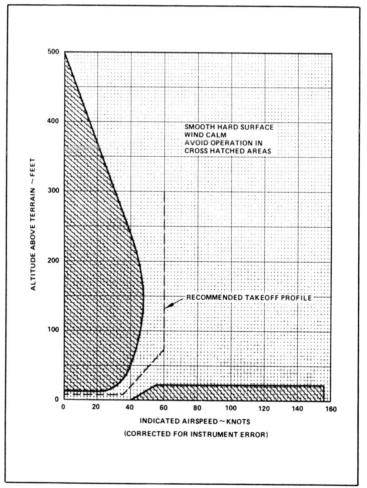

Fig. A-9. High velocity diagram.

When aircraft begins to roll, reduce collective to full down. This minimizes blades skipping off the water.

Release safety belt and shoulder harness.

When rotor blades have stopped turning, clear aircraft as quickly as possible.

Ditching - Power On

Descend to hovering attitude over water.

Unlatch doors.

Passengers and copilot exit aircraft.

Fly a safe distance away from all personnel in the water to avoid injury.

Turn battery and generator switches OFF.

Close twist grip to cutoff position.

Allow aircraft to settle in a level attitude, apply full collective.

When aircraft begins to roll, reduce collective to full down. This minimizes blades skipping off the water.

Release safety belt and shoulder harness.

When rotor blades have stopped turning, clear aircraft as quickly as possible.

Fuel Control or Power Turbine Governor Failure

Failure is indicated by an instrument needle fluctuation, or a rise or drop of N_1, N_2, TOT, or torque.

Failure producing an overspeed: attempt to control rpm by use of the twist grip.

Uncontrollable overspeed: shut down the engine; make an autorotational landing.

Caution

Immediate pilot action is necessary because engine torque, TOT, N_2, and rotor rpm may suddenly increase beyond approved limits. When shutting down the engine, do not reduce collective pitch until the rotor rpm has decreased to within the normal operating range.

Failure producing an underspeed: level-flight is possible if sufficient power is available; When power is insufficient for level flight, make an autorotational landing.

Power turbine governor surge: beep N_2 to full high and reduce twist grip to 103 percent N_2.

Note

This action takes the governor out of the system and should eliminate the surge.

Tail Rotor Failure

Failure is normally indicated by an uncontrollable (by pedal) yawing to the right.

Note

Different types of failure may require a slightly different technique for optimum success in recovery.

General corrective action: reduce power by lowering collective; change speed to 50- to 60-knot range; use left lateral stick in combination with collective pitch to limit left sideslip to a reasonable angle.

Tail rotor or tail rotor drive shaft failure: if conditions permit, place the twist grip in the ground idle position, once a landing site is selected; accomplish a run-on landing at approximately 30 knots.

Hover/low altitude operation: place twist grip in ground idle and perform hovering autorotation following loss of the tail rotor.

One-Way Lock Failure Warning Indications

Malfunction is indicated by an aft feedback in the cyclic stick at high speed.

Note

If one-way lock (feedback control in the longitudinal cyclic system) has a check valve or push rod shaft seizure in the closed valve position, a pull or push of 10 to 20 pounds is required to open the hydraulic relief valve and by pass the check valve. This additional pull or push is required for EACH subsequent longitudinal movement of the cyclic stick. Temporary forces as high as 40 pounds may be experienced in turbulent atmospheric conditions.

Motion required is only that required to safely fly the helicopter; no abnormal or severe maneuvers are necessary. Recommended airspeed with a one-way lock failure is 100 knots IAS or less.

Cyclic Trim Failure

Failure is indicated by an inability to reduce cyclic forces with cyclic trim switch. Failure may be either a frozen or uncontrollable runaway of the trim actuator in either the longitudinal or lateral direction. Runaway to full travel can produce stick forces of approximately 30 pounds in the direction of the runaway.

Avoid rapid and/or abrupt maneuvers.

Establish flight conditions that produce the least cyclic control force.

Trim fails to full forward position: Do not hover downwind; accomplish landing into wind.

Air Restart - Engine

Caution

Do not attempt restart if malfunction is suspected. At low altitude or where time is critical: twist grip in cutoff position; immediately actuate starter.

Note

Depressing the starter button actuates the igniter. If N_1 is 18 percent or above, open twist grip immediately to ground idle. N_1 speeds of 25 to 40 percent are preferred for coolest and fastest relights. Maintain safe autorotational airspeed.

When altitude and time permit: proceed with normal engine start, if N_1 has decayed below 18 percent; recommended airspeed is approximately 60 knots IAS; recommended pressure altitude is 16,000 feet or below; set generator switch and all engine bleeds (heater, filter bleed, and anti-ice) OFF; twist grip in cutoff position; actuate starter; after N_1 reaches steady level (18 to 22 percent) and TOT is 150°C or below, advance twist grip to ground idle.

MALFUNCTIONS

Caution and Warning Lights

The light panel is located at the top of the instrument panel (Fig. A-10).

The battery temperature lights are located above and to the left of the light panel.

The lights will illuminate when a condition other than normal exists.

Red Warning Lights

Engine out: blinking red light; pulsating sound from warning horn and in the headset, if installed.

Low rotor speed: blinking Engine Out light; pulsating sound from warning horn and in the headset, if installed.

Transmission oil pressure/temperature: red lights/lights; land as soon as possible; temperature has exceeded the maximum limit; pressure has dropped below minimum limit.

Battery overtemp, 160°F and above: red light illuminated; turn battery switch off; land as soon as possible.

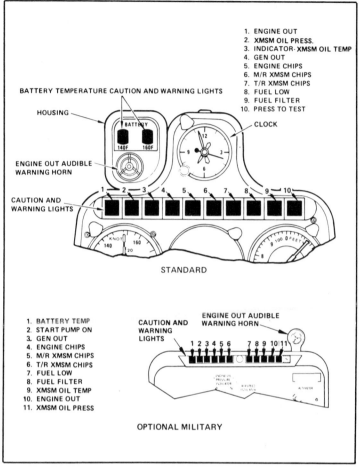

Fig. A-10. Caution and warning lights.

Note

Inspect battery in accordance with the manufacturer's instructions upon landing. No further flights are authorized until battery is inspected.

If proper equipment exists, disconnect and remove battery from aircraft.

Warning

An overheated battery can cause burns to personnel unless protective clothing and adequate tools are utilized. In some instances, the battery may cause a secondary fire or may rupture, adding the further danger of electrolyte burns.

Exercise caution in dealing with an overheated battery. Maintain fire extinguisher ready for use. The use of the fire extinguisher to cool the battery is not recommended.

Amber Caution Lights

Battery overtemp 140°F or above: amber light is illuminated; Turn battery switch OFF.

Note

When the amber light goes out, the battery has cooled to below 140°F.

The battery is to remain off-line during remainder of the flight.

Note

Inspect battery in accordance with the manufacturer's instructions upon landing. No further flights are authorized until battery is inspected.

Generator: Amber light illuminated; ammeter indicating zero; turn generator switch OFF, then ON to reset; if light stays on or comes back on, pull generator circuit breaker (generator switch is still on);

Note

The generator switch in the ON position allows the engine power out warning system to remain operational.

Reduce electrical load to minimum.

Chip detectors: Amber light/lights illuminated; land as soon as possible; the illuminated light indicates possible internal deterioration of the engine, main or tail rotor transmission.

Fuel low: amber light is illuminated; land as soon as possible;

Caution

Sideslips may cause fuel starvation. Avoid large, steady sideslip angles, uncoordinated maneuvers, or speeds above 130 knots IAS.

Never use the light as a working indication of fuel quantity.

The illuminated light indicates there is approximately 35 pounds of fuel remaining in the tank (27 pounds usable).

Fuel filter: amber light is illuminated; monitor the engine instruments and continue the flight;

Caution

If any unusual indications or conditions occur, land as soon as possible.

The illuminated lamp indicates that the pressure through the filter is 0.8 psi differential or more; service the fuel filter prior to the next flight.

NORMAL PROCEDURES

Preflight Requirements

Have a thorough understanding of operating limitations.

Service the helicopter as required. (Refer to Aircraft Handling, Servicing, and Maintenance.)

Determine that the helicopter loading is within limits.

Check the helicopter performance data.

Determine that a Daily Inspection (in accordance with the *Handbook of Maintenance Instructions*) has been accomplished within 24 hours prior to the first flight of each day.

Perform a pilot's preflight inspection prior to each flight (Fig. A-11).

Engine Start

Cyclic stick - neutral   RECHECK

Caution

Damage to rotor head and controls can result if engine start is attempted with cyclic stick in positions other than neutral.

Fuel shut-off valve - open   RECHECK
Cabin heat, engine anti-ice - off   RECHECK
Rotors   CLEARED
Start pump   OPTIONAL
Start/ignition button   PRESS AND HOLD

Note

Starter time limits area: 1 minute ON, 1 minute OFF, 1 minute ON, and 23 minutes OFF.

Twist grip to ground idle to ignite when N_1 indicates 12 and 15 percent (see minimum N_1 Speed Starting Recommendations placard).   ROTATE

Note

When N_1 peaks above 15 percent, rotate twist grip to ground idle to ignite. Peaking of N_1 below 15 percent may occur during cold weather starting conditions; under these conditions, a start may be attempted at a minimum of 12 percent N_1. APU starts are recommended when normal cranking speed cannot be obtained using the battery.

Observe TOT indicator for immediate temperature rise; if no TOT is noted, abort engine start.

Caution

During starts, an overtemperature for a period not to exceed 10 seconds with a momentary peak of 1 second maximum, up to 927°C is permitted. Consult *Allison Engine Operation and Maintenance Manual* if limits are exceeded. If main rotor is not rotating by 25 percent of gas producer speed (N_1), abort the start.

In the event of an aborted start, or a restart soon after shutdown, proceed as follows: close twist grip (cutoff); using starter, continue to motor engine for at least 10 seconds or until TOT is no more than 150°C. (N_1 may exceed the normal ignite speed of 12 to 15 percent.)

Start/ignition button-release at 58 to 60 percent N_1 RELEASE
Engine oil pressure - 50 to 130 psi minimum   CHECK
All warning and caution lights out   CHECK

Note
Transmission warning light OUT within 30 seconds of engine light-off. With the generator switch OFF, the caution light will remain ON.

Engine idle speed 64 to 65 percent N_1 CHECK

Note
During engine operation at ground idle, pedal bungee will tend to depress left pedal, thereby decreasing N_2/N_R speed if pedals are not neutralized.

All other engine instruments: CHECK
N_2 engine and rotor rpm indicators for coincidental reading.

Caution
Malfunctions are indicated if rotor and engine rpm indicator needles are not superimposed. Shut down engine if this condition exists.

Start pump   ON or OFF (PILOT'S DISCRETION)

Engine Run-Up

Note
Avoid continuous operation of engine between 85 and 98 percent N_2.

Electrical power: SELECT
BATT start; set generator switch in ON position, warning light OUT.

EXT start; BATT-EXT switch to BATT after external power source shutdown and disconnect.

Set generator switch in ON position (the warning light will go OUT).

NAV/COM as required   ON AND CHECK
Twist grip   FULL OPEN

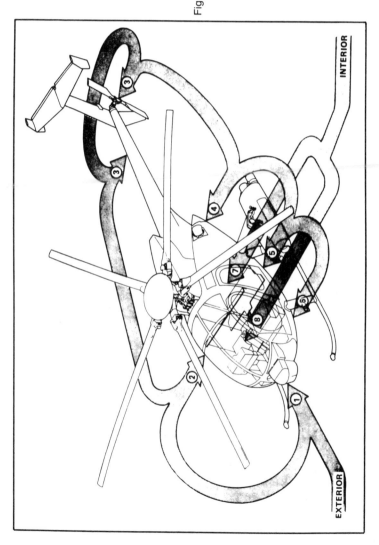

Fig. A-11. Pilot's preflight guide.

195

Note

Avoid rapid acceleration when parked on slippery surface.

If the engine has been shut down for more than 15 minutes, stabilize at idle for one minute before increasing power.

Engine controls: CHECK

N_2 high beep range, 104 percent or more
N_2 low beep range, 98 percent or less

Note

If malfunction is noted, shut down engine.

Low rotor warning - on at 98 ± 1 percent	CHECK
N_2 102 percent	ADJUST
Engine oil pressure above 90 psi	RECHECK
Ammeter	READING

Note

Reading will fluctuate slightly when anticollision light is operating.

All warning lights OUT   RECHECK

Before Takeoff

Flight control friction	RELEASE AND SET AS DE-SIRED
Cyclic trim controls	ADJUST AS DESIRED
One-way lock operation	CHECK
With collective pitch full down, gently move cyclic stick; observe rotor tip for correct movement and track.	CHECK
All instruments in the green	CHECK
Position, anticollision lights	AS REQUIRED
Pitot head (if installed)	AS REQUIRED
Use engine anti-icing when OAT is below 5°C and visible moisture conditions prevail.	ON

Takeoff

Determine hover area and takeoff path are clear.

Follow normal helicopter takeoff procedure with the engine speed at 102 to 103 percent N_2 (Figs. A-12, A-13).

Governed N_2 rpm may increase on takeoff; adjust as necessary to maintain N_2 at 103 percent.

Follow recommended takeoff profile shown on Height Velocity Diagram (refer back to Fig. A-9).

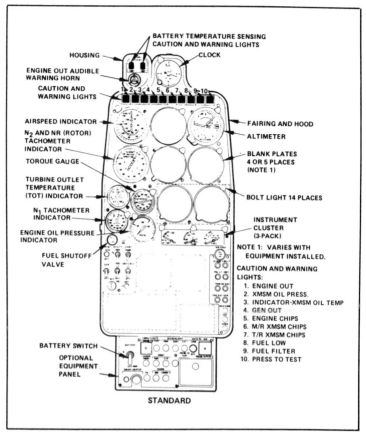

Fig. A-12. Instrument panel I.

Note

A momentary fluctuation in indicated airspeed may occur during acceleration and climbout. This fluctuation is characterized by a rapid rise in indicated airspeed to approximately 40 knots, followed by a drop back to 30 knots and then a normal increase as determined by the rate of acceleration. The recommended takeoff profile will minimize the occurrence of the fluctuation. Indicated airspeed is unreliable when climbing at airspeeds below 40 knots.

Use cyclic trim as desired.

Note

Proper longitudinal trim is established when small fore and aft movements of the cyclic stick require the same force.

Cruise

Trim, using proper trimming procedures described for climbing.

At more than 50 knots and 50-foot altitude above the terrain select N_2 between 102 and 103 percent for the best comfort level.

Use engine anti-icing when OAT is below 5°C (41°F) and visible moisture conditions prevail.

Low Speed Maneuvering

Maneuvers which will exceed the thrust capability of the tail rotor should be avoided.

Note

These limits are normally not encountered, but certain conditions can induce them. Contributing factors are high gross weight, high collective pitch (particularly at a high density altitude) with an ensuing rpm loss, and rapid pedal turns that place the ship in a downwind condition.

Any maneuver that requires full pedal should be avoided.

When performing "crop dusting" turns, it is recommended that only coordinated turns be performed.

Note

Pedal turns during this maneuver should be avoided when operating at or near forward center of gravity limits since aft cycle control may be limited under these special conditions.

When hovering with wind from left, expect random yaw oscillations; with wind from right, expect random pitch and roll oscillations in winds 10 knots and above.

Practice Autorotation

Practice autorotation should not be accomplished if the low fuel warning light is on. If, while in practice autorotation, the low fuel warning light comes on, return to powered flight.

Note

Collective pitch may have to be adjusted upward after establishing autorotation to prevent rotor overspeed if the flight is being conducted at maximum gross weight or at a high density altitude. To reduce sink rate or to extend gliding distance, operate at ...inimum rpm; restore rotor rpm by lowering collective prior to flare-out.

Practice autorotation landings are made as follows:

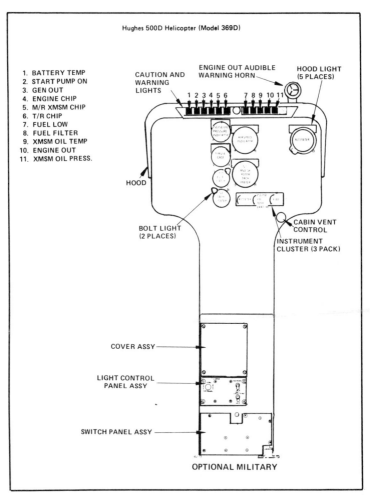

Fig. A-13. Instrument panel II.

For autorotation descent, the twist grip may be in any position. However, if practice autorotation landing (minimum engine power) is desired, rotate the twist grip to the idle position;

If power recovery is desired, the twist grip must be rotated to maximum to make full engine power available upon demand;

Practice autorotations should be conducted at 131 knots IAS or below (see V_{NE} placards). Maintain rotor speed between 410 and 523 rpm by use of collective control;

Maximum gliding distance is obtained at 80 knots/410 rotor rpm;

199

Minimum rate of descent is obtained at 60 knots/410 rotor rpm.

Touch down is a level attitude.

Avoid the use of aft cyclic stick or rapid lowering of the collective pitch during initial ground contact or during ground slide.

Note

Normal rotor rpm (full down collective) is 485 ± rpm at 2250-pound gross weight at sea level, 60 knots IAS. The rpm will decrease 10 for each 100-pound reduction in gross weight and increase 6.5 for each 1000-foot increase in density altitude. For gross weights greater than 2250 pounds, increase collective control as required to maintain approximately 485 rpm.

Landing Approach

Set N_2 at 103 percent.

Running Landing

Maximum recommended ground contact speed for smooth, hard surface is 30 knots.

Avoid rapid lowering of collective pitch control after ground contact.

Avoid use of aft cyclic after ground contact.

Engine/Aircraft Shutdown

Collective stick	FULL DOWN, APPLY FRICTION

Caution

Do not use collective pitch to slow rotor

Cyclic stick	NEUTRAL
Pedals (maintain until rotor has stopped turning)	CENTERED
Twist grip in GROUND IDLE detent - hold for two minutes	SET
Twist grip from ground idle stop to CUTOFF position	SET

Note

To ensure throttle cutoff, hold twist grip in cutoff position until N_1 decelerates to zero and TOT is stabilized. Check for TOT decrease.

Engine out warning at 55 percent N_1	CHECK
Generator switch	OFF
Fuel shutoff valve	CLOSED (PILOT'S DISCRETION)
NAV/COM switches	OFF
All other switches	OFF
BATT/EXT switch	OFF
Cyclic stick	NEUTRAL, APPLY FRICTION

Rotor brake (if installed) - apply at 205 rpm or less; release during last rotor revolution

Rotor brake handle stowed UP	APPLY CHECK

Post Flight

Aircraft - investigate any suspected damage	CHECK
Fuel and oil leaks	CHECK
Logbook entries	COMPLETE
Flight manual and equipment	STOWED
Aircraft, tiedowns, covers	SECURED

Normal Engine Restart

Residual TOT should not exceed 150°C when light OFF is attempted. TOT can readily be reduced by motoring engine with the starter. Speeds in excess of 15 percent N_1 may be experienced.

Fuel System

Standard nonself-sealing tanks: Capacity is 64.0 U.S. gallons (242 liters), 416 pounds. Usable fuel is 62.7 U.S. gallons (237 liters), 408 pounds.

Optional self-sealing tanks: Capacity is 62.0 U.S. gallons (234 liters), 402 pounds. Usable fuel is 60.7 U.S. gallons (229 liters), 394 pounds.

PERFORMANCE DATA

Controllability during downwind hovering, sideward and rearward flight has been demonstrated to be adequate in winds up to 17 knots (Figs. A-14, A-15).

Indicated airspeed (IAS) corrected for position and instrument error equals calibrated airspeed (CAS) (Figs. A-16, A-17, A-18).

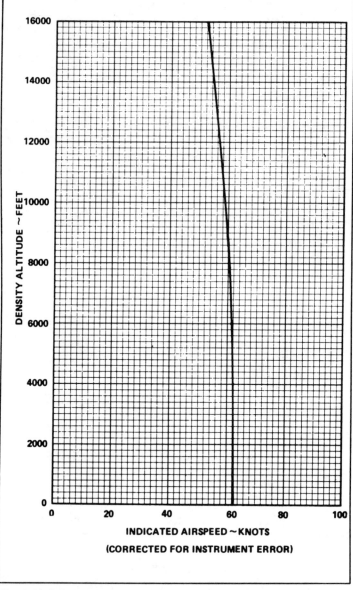

Fig. A-14. Speed for best rate of climb.

To determine if engine power has deteriorated, establish 103 percent N_2, read and note torque pressure, altitude, and OAT while in hover (Fig. A-19).

WEIGHT AND BALANCE DATA
Weight and Balance Characteristics

The weight and balance characteristics of the Hughes 500D Model 369D helicopter are as follows: (Table A-1):

Maximum Certified
  Gross Weight ....3000 pounds
Longitudinal
  Reference Datum ....100 inches forward
                                                  of rotor centerline
                                             (rotor hub centerline
                                                is located at Sta-
                                                 tion 100) (Figs.
                                                   A-20, A-21,
                                                   A-22, A-23).
Cargo Deck Capacity ....1300 pounds (not to
                                                  exceed 115 pounds
                                                    per square foot)

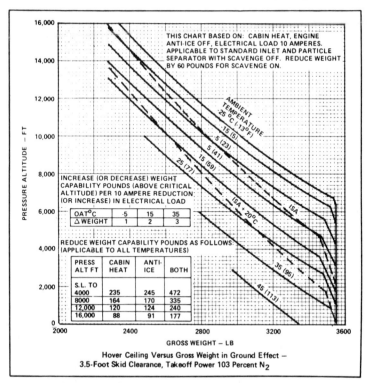

Fig. A-15. Hover ceiling/gross weight in ground effect.

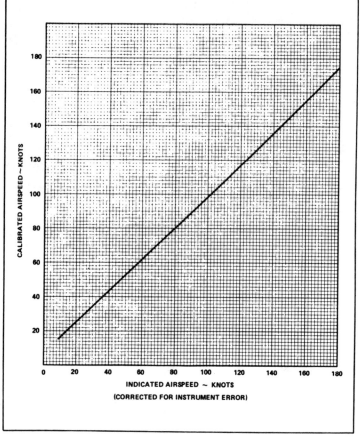

Fig. A-16. Airspeed calibration curve.

Utility Stowage
    Compartment ....Limited to 50 pounds

    Center of gravity limits: lateral "+" is right of centerline, lateral "−" is left of centerline when looking forward.

Load Limits and Balance Criteria

    The Hughes 500D Model 369D helicopter is designed for the limit loads and balance conditions noted in Table 3-1. These limitations must not be exceeded at any time during flight.

    The delivered weight (the term "delivered weight" includes oil and unusable fuel), recorded in the Weight and Balance Record inserted in this section, shall be used to perform all weight and balance computations (Figs. A-24, A-25).

Equipment Removal or Installation

Removal or addition of equipment must be entered on the repair and alteration report form FAA 337 in accordance with Civil Air Regulations which shall then become part of the helicopter file.

The weight and balance effects of these changes must also be recorded in the Weight and Balance Record inserted in this section.

The balance and station diagrams shown in Figs. A-21 through A-23 can be used as an aid for weight and balance changes.

Weight and Balance Determination - Passenger Configuration

To determine that the gross weight and longitudinal center of gravity (fore and aft) for a given flight are within limits, proceed as follows:

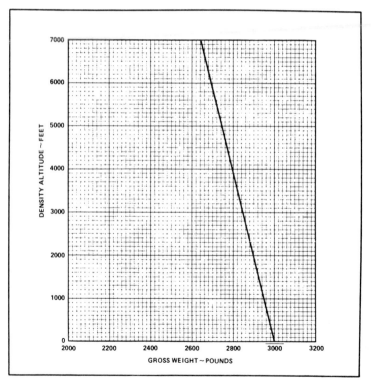

Fig. A-17. Gross weight limits for height velocity diagram.

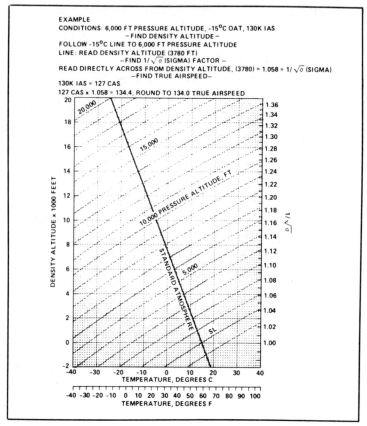

EXAMPLE
CONDITIONS: 6,000 FT PRESSURE ALTITUDE, -15°C OAT, 130K IAS
– FIND DENSITY ALTITUDE –
FOLLOW -15°C LINE TO 6,000 FT PRESSURE ALTITUDE
LINE: READ DENSITY ALTITUDE (3780 FT)
– FIND 1/√σ (SIGMA) FACTOR –
READ DIRECTLY ACROSS FROM DENSITY ALTITUDE, (3780) = 1.058 = 1/√σ (SIGMA)
– FIND TRUE AIRSPEED–
130K IAS = 127 CAS
127 CAS × 1.058 = 134.4; ROUND TO 134.0 TRUE AIRSPEED

Fig. A-18. Density altitude chart.

Obtain the aircraft delivered weight and moment from the Weight and Balance Record inserted in this section; determine weights and moments of useful load items (Fig. A-26; Tables A-2 throught A-4). Add the above items (Table A-1).

Calculation of Longitudinal CG

CG (Zero Fuel Weight):

$$\frac{\text{Moment at Zero Fuel Weight}}{\text{Zero Fuel Weight}} = \frac{240{,}202}{2{,}389} = 100.5 \text{ in.}$$

CG (Gross Weight):

$$\frac{\text{Moment at Gross Weight}}{\text{Gross Weight}} = \frac{280{,}896}{2{,}805} = 100.1 \text{ in.}$$

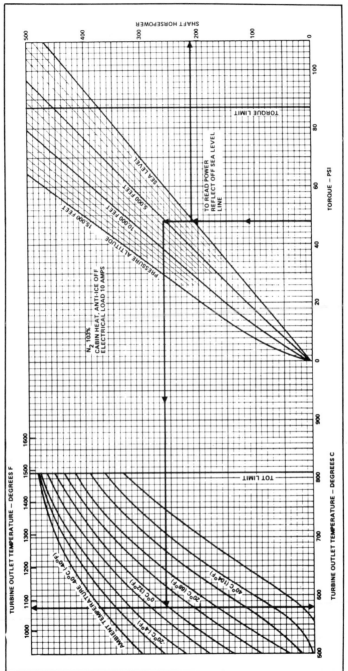

Fig. A-19. Engine power check chart, Allison 250-C20B engine.

Table A-1. Center of Gravity Limits.

Gross Weight (lb)	Longitudinal CG Limit (Sta-in)		Lateral CG Limit (Sta-in)
	Forward	Aft*	(+) Right, (−) Left
3000	99.0	103.0	±3.0
2500	99.0	104.5	±3.0
2000	99.0	106.0	±3.0
1538	99.0	107.4	±3.0

*NOTE: The aft longitudinal CG limit varies linearly from a gross weight of 3000 pounds at Station 103.0 to 1538 pounds at Station 107.4.

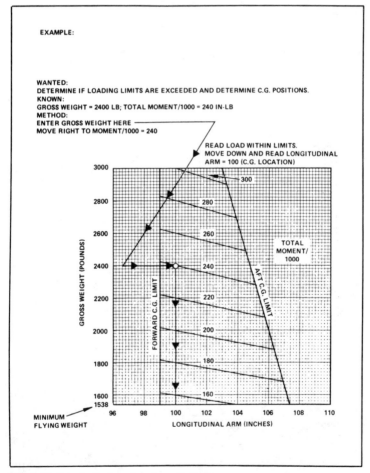

Fig. A-20. Longitudinal center of gravity limits.

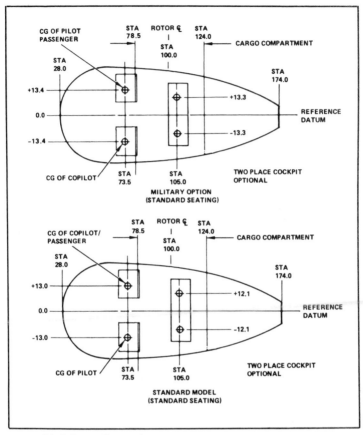

Fig. A-21. Balance diagram I.

The CGs fall within the limits specified; therefore, the loading meets the longitudinal CG requirements.

If loadings are not symmetrical about aircraft centerline, determine the lateral CGs.

Caution

Gross weight must not exceed 3000 pounds.

Longitudinal Loading of Cargo

The large aft compartment of the Model 369D provides great flexibility in the variety of cargo loads it can accommodate.

In general, the placement of cargo CG within four inches of the center of the compartment will ensure that the helicopter will be within the approved CG limits.

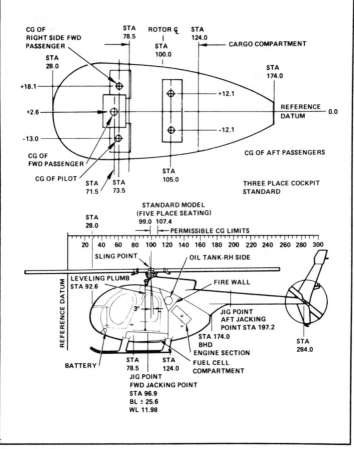

Fig. A-22. Balance diagram II.

To determine the gross weight and center of gravity for a given flight are within limits, proceed as follows: establish the weight of the cargo load; determine the location of the cargo longitudinal CG, measure the distance to the cargo from the jacking point located on the side of the fuselage (Station 96.9).

Cargo CG = 96.9 ± measured distance (inches); i.e., + if aft of mark, − if forward of mark.

Obtain the cargo moment: Cargo Moment = Cargo Weight x Cargo CG

Perform weight and balance as previously described for passenger configuration.

Calculation of Longitudinal CG

CG (Zero Fuel Weight):

$$\frac{\text{Moment at Zero Fuel Weight}}{\text{Zero Fuel Weight}} = \frac{266{,}847}{2{,}619} = 101.9 \text{ in.}$$

CG (Gross Weight):

$$\frac{\text{Moment at Gross Weight}}{\text{Gross Weight}} = \frac{303{,}847}{3{,}000} = 101.3 \text{ in.}$$

Note

The CGs fall within the limits specified; therefore, the loading meets the longitudinal CG requirements. Then, determine the lateral CGs.

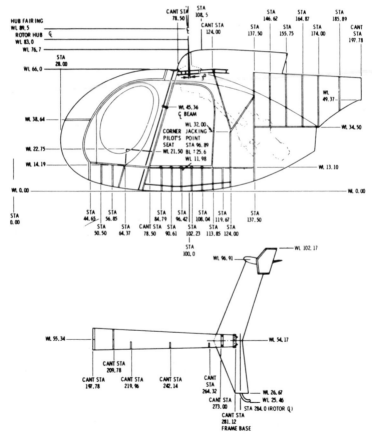

Fig. A-23. Station diagram.

WEIGHT AND BALANCE REPORT
MODEL 500D (369D)

WEIGHED BY ____J. DOE____   DATE ___6-15-77___

REGISTRATION NO. ___09872F___   SERIAL NO. ___47-0137D___   MODEL ___369D___

WEIGHING POINTS	SCALE READING (LBS)	TARE OR CALIBRATION CORRECTION (LBS)	NET WEIGHT (LBS)	ARM (IN.)	MOMENT (IN. LB)
LEFT MAIN	784.7	136.3	648.4	96.9	62830
RIGHT MAIN	777.2	135.4	641.8	96.9	62190
TAIL	359.3	177.7	181.6	197.2	35811
TOTAL UNADJUSTED NET WEIGHT			1471.8	109.2	160831

MOMENT ARM OF MAIN REACTION   96.9

MOMENT ARM OF TAIL REACTION   197.2

FUEL/OIL ABOARD AT TIME OF WEIGHING

MISSING EQUIPMENT AT TIME OF WEIGHING			
ITEM	WEIGHT (LBS)	ARM (IN.)	MOMENT (IN.-LB)
FLIGHT MANUAL	1.0	85.0	85
TOTAL	1.0	85.0	85

SURPLUS EQUIPMENT AT TIME OF WEIGHING			
ITEM	WEIGHT (LBS)	ARM (IN.)	MOMENT (IN.-LB)
JACK FITTINGS	1.3	96.9	126
TOTAL	1.3	96.9	126

Fig. A-24. Sample Weight and Balance Report I.

Caution
Gross weight must not exceed 3000 pounds.

Permissible Lateral Loadings - Passenger Configuration

The safe operation of this helicopter requires that it be flown within the established lateral as well as longitudinal center of gravity limits.

It is therefore imperative that lateral center of gravity control be exercised.

All combinations of passenger loadings are permissible if gross weight, longitudinal, and lateral center of gravity considerations permit.

For passenger lateral center of gravity, refer to Figs. A-21 and A-22, and Table A-1.

Lateral Loading of Cargo

To ensure that the lateral center of gravity of the helicopter remains within the prescribed limits throughout the entire flight,

WEIGHT AND C.G. CALCULATIONS			
	WEIGHT (LBS)	ARM (IN.)	MOMENT (IN. LB)
TOTAL UNADJUSTED NET WEIGHT	1471.8	109.3	160,831
TOTAL WEIGHT OF MISSING EQUIPMENT	+ 1.0	85.0	+ 85
TOTAL WEIGHT OF SURPLUS EQUIPMENT	− 1.3	96.9	− 126
TOTAL DELIVERED WEIGHT	1471.5	109.3	160,790

REFER TO THE OWNER'S MANUAL FOR C.G. LIMITS APPLICABLE FOR GROSS WEIGHT RANGE.

EXAMPLES OF FORWARD AND AFT LOADING

EXAMPLE 1, FORWARD	WEIGHT (LBS)	ARM (IN.)	MOMENT (IN. LB)
TOTAL DELIVERED WEIGHT	1471.5	109.3	160,790
PILOT	170.0	73.5	12,495
PASSENGER – FWD CENTER	170.0	71.5	12,155
PASSENGER – FWD	170.0	73.5	12,495
CRITICAL FUEL QUANTITY – FWD	40.0	90.6	3624
GROSS WEIGHT (CRITICAL FUEL) – FWD C.G.	2021.5	99.7	201,559

APPROVED FWD C.G. LIMIT FOR EXAMPLE 1 GROSS WEIGHT __99.0__ INCHES.

EXAMPLE 2, AFT	WEIGHT (LBS)	ARM (IN.)	MOMENT (IN. LB)
TOTAL DELIVERED WEIGHT	1471.5	109.3	160,790
PILOT	170.0	73.5	12,495
PASSENGER – AFT L.H.	170.0	105.0	17,850
PASSENGER – AFT R.H.	170.0	105.0	17,850
BAGGAGE – UNDER SEAT	50.0	110.0	5,500
GROSS WEIGHT (ZERO FUEL) – AFT C.G.	2031.5	105.6	214,485

APPROVED AFT C.G. LIMIT FOR EXAMPLE 2 GROSS WEIGHT __*__ INCHES.

*NOTE: SEE OWNER'S MANUAL, SECTION 6, FIGURE 1 FOR AFT CG LIMIT AT GROSS WEIGHT 42031.5 POUNDS = 105.9 INCHES.

Fig. A-25. Sample Weight and Balance Report II.

DELIVERED WEIGHT AND BALANCE RECORD
(CONTINUOUS HISTORY OF CHANGES IN STRUCTURE OR EQUIPMENT AFFECTING WEIGHT AND BALANCE)

AIRCRAFT MODEL	SERIAL NUMBER	REGISTRATION NUMBER
369D	47-0137D	09872F

DATE	ITEM NO.		DESCRIPTION OF ARTICLE OR MODIFICATION	WEIGHT CHANGE						RUNNING TOTAL BASIC AIRCRAFT		
	IN	OUT		ADDED (+)			REMOVED (−)					
				WEIGHT	ARM	MOMENT† In-Lb	WEIGHT	ARM	MOMENT† In-Lb	WEIGHT	ARM	MOMENT† IN.-LB.
8-12-77			Total Delivered Weight							1471.5	109.3	160,790

†ENTER CONSTANT USED BELOW LINE

FORM 985

Fig. A-26. Delivered Weight and Balance Record.

214

Items	Weight (lb)	Moment (in-lb)
Delivered Weight	1,471	160,790
Oil, Engine	8	1,067
Pilot	170	12,495
Passenger - Fwd Outboard	170	12,495
Passenger - Fwd Center	170	12,155
Passenger - Aft R/H	170	17,850
Passenger - Aft L/H	170	17,850
Utility Stowage (Station 55)	20	1,100
Baggage (under seat)	40	4,400
1. Zero Fuel Weight	2,389	240,202
Fuel	416	40,694
2. Gross Weight	2,805	280,896

the cargo center of gravity should be located within four inches of the center of the compartment. (Fig. A-27, Table A-5 through A-7).

To determine that the gross weight and lateral center of gravity for a given flight are within limits, proceed as follows: establish the weight of the cargo load; determine the lateral location of cargo center of gravity. Measure the cargo distance from centerline of aircraft (lateral station zero), right (+), left (−).

Table A-3. Weights and Moments.

Items	Weight (lb)	Moment (in-lb)
Delivered Weight	1,471	160,790
Oil	8	1,067
Pilot	170	12,495
Passenger - Fwd Outboard	170	12,495
Cargo	800	80,000
1. Zero Fuel Weight	2,619	266,847
Fuel	381	37,000
2. Gross Weight	3,000	303,847

Table A-4. Weights and Moments.

Items	Weight (lb)	Lateral Arm (in)	Lateral Moment (in-lb)
Delivered Weight	1,471	0	0
Oil	8	+10.0	+ 80
Pilot (L/H)	170	− 13.0	− 2,210
Passenger - Fwd (R/H)	170	+18.1	+3,077
Cargo	800	+ 2.0	+1,600
1. Zero Fuel Weight	2,619	+ 1.0	+2,547
Add Fuel	381	0	0
2. Gross Weight	3,000	+ 0.8	+2,547

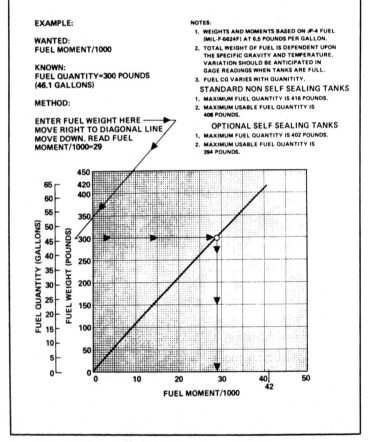

EXAMPLE:

WANTED:
FUEL MOMENT/1000

KNOWN:
FUEL QUANTITY=300 POUNDS
(46.1 GALLONS)

METHOD:

ENTER FUEL WEIGHT HERE →
MOVE RIGHT TO DIAGONAL LINE
MOVE DOWN. READ FUEL
MOMENT/1000=29

NOTES:
1. WEIGHTS AND MOMENTS BASED ON JP-4 FUEL (MIL-F-5624F) AT 6.5 POUNDS PER GALLON.
2. TOTAL WEIGHT OF FUEL IS DEPENDENT UPON THE SPECIFIC GRAVITY AND TEMPERATURE. VARIATION SHOULD BE ANTICIPATED IN GAGE READINGS WHEN TANKS ARE FULL.
3. FUEL CG VARIES WITH QUANTITY.

STANDARD NON SELF SEALING TANKS
1. MAXIMUM FUEL QUANTITY IS 416 POUNDS.
2. MAXIMUM USABLE FUEL QUANTITY IS 408 POUNDS.

OPTIONAL SELF SEALING TANKS
1. MAXIMUM FUEL QUANTITY IS 402 POUNDS.
2. MAXIMUM USABLE FUEL QUANTITY IS 394 POUNDS.

Fig. A-27. Fuel Moment (JP-4 at 6.5 pounds per gallon).

Table A-5. Weights and Longitudinal Moments—Pilots, Passenger, Baggage.

Pilot and Passenger Weights and Longitudinal Moments			
Passenger Weight (lb)	Moment Pilot or Fwd R/H Passenger	Moment Center Fwd Passenger	Moment Aft Passenger R/H and L/H
120	8,820	8,580	12,600
140	10,290	10,010	14,700
160	11,760	11,440	16,800
170	12,495	12,155	17,850
180	13,230	12,870	18,900
200	14,700	14,300	21,000
220	16,170	15,730	23,100
240	17,640	17,160	25,200

Baggage Weights and Longitudinal Moments			
Baggage Weight (lb)	Moment Under Seat and Center Station 110	Moment Behind Seat Station 120	Moment Fwd Bulkhead Station 87
10	1,100	1,200	870
20	2,200	2,400	1,740
30	3,300	3,600	2,610
40	4,400	4,800	3,480
50	5,500	6,000	4,350
60	6,600	7,200	5,220
70	7,700	8,400	6,090
80	8,800	9,600	6,960
90	9,900	10,800	7,830
100	11,000	12,000	8,700

Obtain the lateral cargo moment as follows: Lateral Cargo Moment = Cargo Weight x Lateral Cargo CG. Perform weight and balance as previously described for longitudinal CG determination.

Calculation of Lateral CG

CG (Zero Fuel Weight):

$$\frac{\text{Moment at Zero Fuel Weight}}{\text{Zero Fuel Weight}} = \frac{+2,547}{2,617} = 1.0 \text{ in.}$$

CG (Gross Weight):

$$\frac{\text{Moment at Gross Weight}}{\text{Gross Weight}} = \frac{+2,547}{3,000} = +0.8 \text{ in.}$$

Table A-6. Aft Compartment Passenger Weights and Longitudinal Moments.

Passenger(s) (lb)	Moment (in-lb)	
	Fwd Position (Sta 95.5)	Aft Position (Sta 109.2)
150	14,300	16,400
175	16,700	19,100
200	19,100	21,800
225	21,500	24,600
250	23,900	27,300
275	26,300	30,000
300	28,700	32,800
325	31,000	35,500
350	33,400	38,200
375	35,800	41,000
400	38,200	43,700

Note

The determined lateral CGs of +1.0 inch at 2619 pounds and +0.8 inch at 3000 pounds fall within the lateral limits.

Caution

Gross weight must not exceed 3000 pounds.

Table A-7. Cargo Weight versus Loop Requirement.

Number of Required Restraint Loops			
Cargo (lb)	Forward Restraint	Aft Restraint	Vertical/ Lateral Restraint
Up to 100	1	1	2
101 to 300	2	1	2
301 to 400	3	2	2
401 to 600	4	2	2
601 to 800	5	3	2
801 to 1000	6	3	3
1001 to 1100	7*	4	3
1101 to 1200	8*	4	3
1201 to 1300	8*	4	3
*Note the 7th and 8th loops are to use the outboard seat belt attach fitting (Station 124).			

Internal Cargo Loading

The following should be adhered to when carrying cargo internally: rope, cable, or equivalent must have a minimum loop strength of 1800 pounds. Restrain the cargo from shifting, using the correct number of restraining loops in accordance with Tables A-5 through A-7. Position restraining loop in accordance with Fig. A-28; cargo deck capacity is 1300 pounds (not to exceed 115 pounds per square foot).

View II shows typical tiedown for 500-pound cargo. Restraint loops are to be secured as indicated and tied to the cargo to prevent slippage of the loops. Variations of the tiedown are allowable, providing total restraint requirements are met.

Caution should be exercised to keep the cargo from bearing against the center slanted portion of the aft bulkhead.

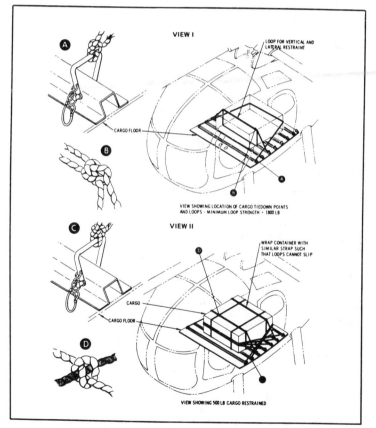

Fig. A-28. Cargo restraint.

Maintenance and Operational Check Requirements and Precautions

All maintenance and operational checks that require operation of helicopter must be performed in accordance with requirements and limitations specified in the Hughes 369D *Pilot's Flight Manual* and any applicable *Optional Equipment Supplements*.

Operational Checks: after performance of maintenance or modification, the affected parts are to be inspected for discrepancies and an operational check is to be performed.

Cautions and Warnings in HMI *(Handbook of Maintenance Instruction):*

Caution and warning statements throughout this manual are provided to promote safe maintenance of the helicopter.

General Information - Inspections: all inspections of a general nature include a visual inspection of the specified system, equipment, or component for cracks, corrosion, distortion, security, and any other obvious defects or damage. Inspections for fuel and oil systems, equipments or components containing or using fuel or oil include checks for leakage, distortion, and clogging, including hoses, lines, tubing, and fittings as applicable.

General Maintenance Data: during maintenance of the helicopter, comply with the following:

At disconnection, cap fuel and oil lines and fittings; remove caps at reconnection.

At removal, discard used O-rings; replace with new O-ring at reassembly or reinstallation.

Helicopter Fundamentals

The major components of the helicopter are shown in Fig. A-29.

Principal dimensions are shown in Fig. A-30.

Reference is occasionally made to "station" and "waterline" throughout the handbook. To assist in locating the components being discussed, refer to the station diagram in the section on Weight and Balance Data. The maximum weights for large components that may require hoisting are listed in Table A-8.

Helicopter Ground Handling

Ground handling of helicopter includes hoisting, jacking, leveling, parking, and mooring (Fig. A-31). The following sections

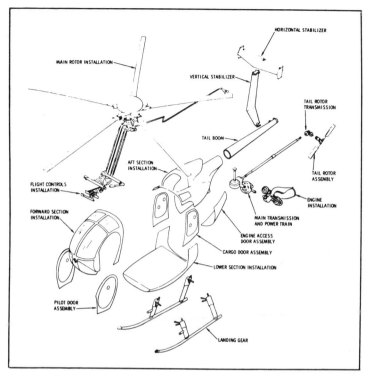

Fig. A-29. 369D Helicopter major components.

present instructions and precautions for all ground handling functions.

Use of External Power

An external receptacle is located at the right side of the pilot's compartment seat structure. The right door must be open to use the receptacle. Any source of external 28-volt, direct-current power with sufficient amperage rating may be used. (Engine starting requirements are approximately 375 amperes minimum.)

Before connecting external power, be sure that helicopter main electrical power selector switch is OFF.

After power is connected to receptacle, power switch must be set at EXT position to connect external power to helicopter electrical system.

Hoisting

Comply with the following precautions during any hoisting operation:

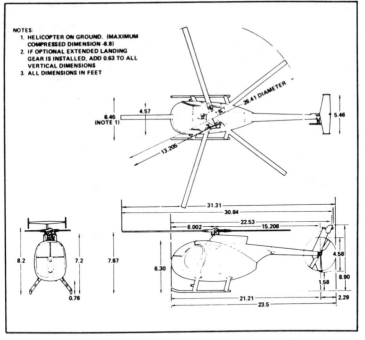

Fig. A-30. 369D helicopter principal dimensions.

Use a hoist of no less than 3500-pound capacity when hoisting complete helicopter. Use hoisting equipment of sufficient capacity (minimum 20 percent over-rate) to hoist heavier components if handled separately. (Table A-8 lists approximate maximum weights.)

Hoisting Procedures: install hoisting adapter on main rotor hub so that hoisting eyebolts fit into slots on hoisting adapter (Fig.

Table A-8. Approximate Maximum Hoisting Weights of Components.

Item	Weight
Tailboom	18
Main rotor hub	85
Main transmission (wet)	106
Engine (built-up)	192
Helicopter (less engine)	1178
Helicopter (less main rotor hub, swashplate, scissors, and rotor blades)	1150
Helicopter (complete)	1370

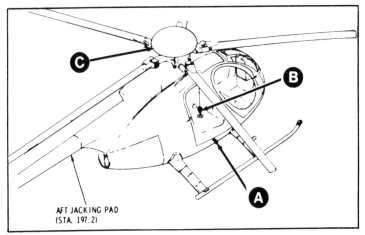

Fig. A-31. Hoisting, jacking, and leveling.

A-32). Install quick-release pins; attach cable from overhead hoist to adapter eye; secure a line to tailboom. Have an assistant hold line to keep helicopter from swinging; hoist slowly and smoothly to maintain steady lifting force.

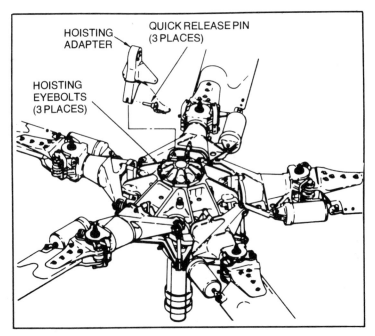

Fig. A-32. Hoisting.

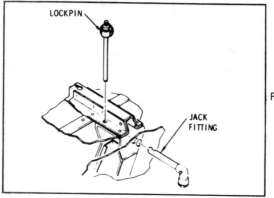

Fig. A-33. Jacking.

Jacking

Provisions for jacking helicopter (Fig. A-33) are provided by two forward (side) jacking point fittings and an aft jacking pad.

Install jack fittings in fuselage jacking points. Secure jack fittings with locking pins located in fuel cell access doors. Place suitable jacks under jack fittings, and under aft jacking pad. Raise helicopter to desired height.

Note

When helicopter is jacked from one side only, a cushioned saddle-type support should be placed under tailboom at aft jacking pad location for extra stability.

Leveling

Leveling (Fig. A-34) is accomplished by positioning helicopter to align a plumb bob with register marks on the target plate on cargo compartment door.

Suspend plumb bob from a line attached to support clip on upper right edge of controls tunnel. Raise helicopter from ground. Adjust side jacks to level helicopter laterally. Adjust tailboom jack to level helicopter longitudinally. Recheck lateral and longitudinal levels until plumb bob exactly aligns with marks on target plate.

Ground Handling Wheels

Standard ground handling wheels (Fig. A-35), available as a special tool, are used for moving helicopter by hand and for towing the helicopter. The wheels are manually lowered with a detachable jack handle and are held in the down position (helicopter raised on wheels) by a mechanical lock.

The wheels are equipped with tow bar attach fittings. Attach ground handling wheels and hold tail up when lowering the wheels (raising helicopter).

At regular intervals, check that wheel tire pressure is 80-90 psi and repack wheel bearings with grease.

Moving and Towing Helicopter

Manually move helicopter on ground handling wheels by balancing at tailboom and pushing on rear fuselage portion of airframe.

Caution

Except under extreme emergency conditions, do not tow helicopter at speeds over 5 mph. Do not allow front end of skid tubes to drag on ground. Avoid sudden stops and starts, and short turns which could cause helicopter to turn over. Allow inside wheel to turn (not pivot) while helicopter is being turned. Safe minimum turning radius is approximately 20 feet.

Tow helicopter on ground handling wheels by attaching suitable tow bar fittings. If two bar is not equipped to keep front ends of

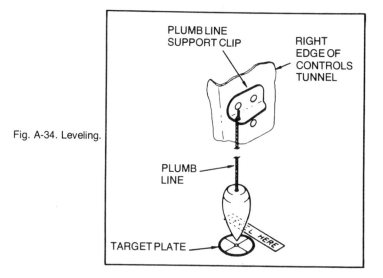

Fig. A-34. Leveling.

PLUMB LINE
SUPPORT CLIP

RIGHT EDGE OF CONTROLS TUNNEL

PLUMB LINE

TARGET PLATE

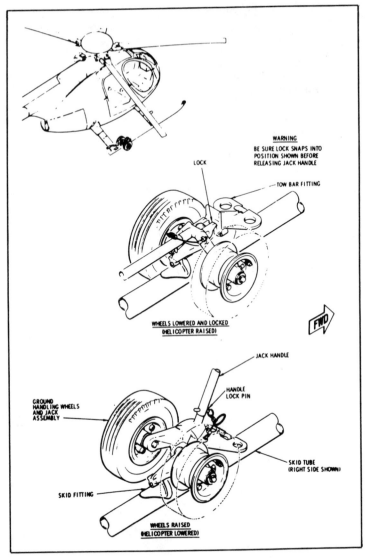

WARNING

BE SURE LOCK SNAPS INTO
POSITION SHOWN BEFORE
RELEASING JACK HANDLE

LOCK

TOW BAR FITTING

WHEELS LOWERED AND LOCKED
(HELICOPTER RAISED)

FWD

JACK HANDLE

HANDLE
LOCK PIN

GROUND
HANDLING WHEELS
AND JACK
ASSEMBLY

SKID TUBE
(RIGHT SIDE SHOWN)

SKID FITTING

WHEELS RAISED
(HELICOPTER LOWERED)

Fig. A-35. Ground handling wheels.

skid tubes from dragging, have an assistant balance helicopter at
tailboom.

Parking

To park helicopter for short intervals, perform following
steps:

Caution

To prevent rotor damage from blade flapping (droop stop pounding) as a result of air turbulence from other aircraft landing, taking off or taxiing or sudden wind gusts, rotor blades should be secured whenever helicopter is parked.

Locate helicopter slightly more than blade clearance from nearby objects on most level ground available; apply friction to lock cyclic stick so that friction control knobs are positioned on lateral and longitudinal travel stop guides as follows: neutral laterally (center of slot), and one-third from full aft longitudinally (one-third up slot).

Note

If not already accomplished, apply paint mark on edge of guide to locate neutral position for future reference.

Secure main rotor blades as follows: turn blades until one blade is directly above tailboom. Install blade socks on all blades. See Figs. A-36 through A-39.

Caution

When securing blade sock tiedown cords, take up slack but do not apply bending loads on blades.

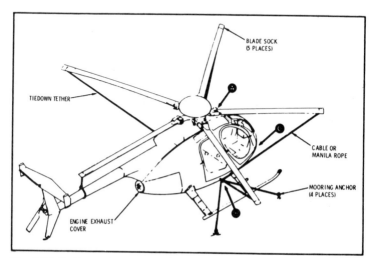

Fig. A-36. Parking and mooring.

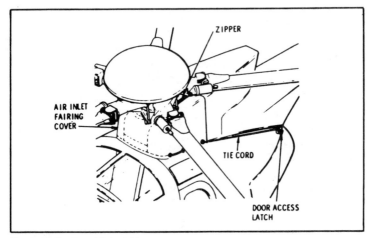

Fig. A-37. Engine air inlet fairing cover.

Secure blade sock tiedown cord for blade located above tail-boom to tailboom. Secure other blade sock tiedown cords to fuse-lage jack fittings.

For longer duration parking, also perform the following steps: install air inlet fairing cover on air inlet front fairing; install engine exhaust cover on exhaust tailpipe.

Mooring

Whenever severe storm conditions or wind velocities higher than 40 knots are forecast, helicopter should be hangared or evacuated to a safer area.

If these precautions are not possible, moor helicopter as follows: park helicopter or remove main rotor blades and install air inlet fairing and engine exhaust covers. Install pitot tube cover; fill fuel tank (if possible); apply friction to lock cyclic and collective sticks; secure helicopter to ground by attaching restraining lines (cable or rope) between jack fittings and stakes or ground anchors.

Servicing

Servicing of helicopter includes replenishment of fuel chang-ing or replenishment of oil and other such maintenance functions.

Fuels, oils, other servicing materials and capacities are listed in Table A-9.

Locations of servicing points are shown in Fig. A-40 through A-42. Comply with the following precautions when servicing the fuel system.

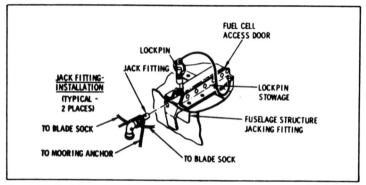

Fig. A-38. Jack fitting installation.

Warning

Turn off electrical switches and disconnect any external power from helicopter. Electrically ground helicopter prior to refueling or defueling. Static discharge spark in presence of fuel vapors can cause fire or an explosion.

Caution

Use extreme care when applying any type of lubrication (grease, oil, dry-film, etc.) in vicinity of Teflon bearings. Most lubricants allow a dirt-retaining film to form or have other detrimental effects that can cause rapid deterioration of bearing surfaces.

Refueling vehicle should be parked a minimum of 20 feet from helicopter during fueling operation.

Before starting fueling operation, always ground fueling nozzle or fuel truck to GROUND HERE receptacle or to another are metal location.

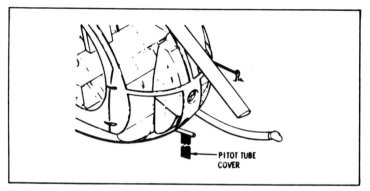

Fig. A-39. Pitot tube cover.

Table A-9. Servicing Materials (Operating Supplies).

Specification	Group	Material	Manufacturer
Item 1. Tail Rotor Transmission - Capacity: 0.5 U.S. Pt (0.23 Liter)			
None (see footnotes 1 and 3)	--	Turbo Oil No. 35	Exxon Co. (formerly Humble Oil and Refining) P.O. Box 2180 Houston, TX 77001
MIL-L-23699	22	Aero Shell Turbine Oil 500	Shell Oil Co. 50 W. 50th Street New York, NY 10020
	21	Mobil Jet II (RM-139A)	Mobil Oil Co. 150 E. 42nd Street New York, NY 10017
Item 2. Main Transmission - Capacity: 12,0 U.S. Pt (5.67 Liters)			
Use the materials listed under item 1.			
Item 3. Engine Oil Tank - Capacity 3.0 U.S. Pt (2.84 Liters)			
MIL-L-7808G	1	American PQ Lubricant 6899	American Oil & Supply Co. 238 Wilson Avenue Newark, NJ 07105
	1	Mobil Avrex S Turbo 256	Mobil Oil Co. 150 E. 42nd Street New York, NY 10017
	4	Brayco 880H	Bray Oil Co. 1925 Marianna St. Los Angeles, CA 90032
	5	Exxon Turbo Oil 2389	Exxon Co. (formerly Humble Oil and Refining P.O. Box 2180 Houston, TX 77001
	9	Stauffer Jet II (Castrol 205)	Stauffer Chemical 380 Madison Ave. New York, NY 10017
MIL-L-23699	21	Mobil Jet II (RM-139A)	Mobil Oil Co.
	22	Aero Shell Turbine Oil 500	Shell Oil Co.
	22	Rayco 899 (C-915)	Royal Lubricants
	23	American PQ Lubricants 6700	American Oil & Supply Co.
	23	Brayco 899G	Bray Oil Company 1925 N. Marianna St. Los Angeles, CA 90032

Specification	Group	Material	Manufacturer
	23	Hatcol 3211	Hatco Chemical Div. W.R. Grace & Co. King George Post Rd. Fords, NJ 08863
	24	Exxon Turbo Oil 2380	Exxon Co. (formerly Humble Oil and Refining)

Item 4. Fuel Tank - Capacity 64.0 U.S. Gal (242 Liters)
  CAUTION: At 4.4°C (40°F) and below, fuel must contain anti-icing additive MIL-I-27686. For blending information refer to Hughes 369D Owners Manual.

  For authorized fuels, refer to Allison Operations and Maintenance Manuals and Allison Commercial Service Letters.

Item 5. Overrunning Clutch - Capacity 1.28 U.S. Oz (38 cc)
  Use the materials listed under item 1.
Item 6. One-Way Lock - Capacity: 0.67 U.S. Oz (20 cc)

Specification	Group	Material	Manufacturer
MIL-H-5606		PQ Hydraulic	American Oil Co.
		Brayco 756C Brayco 756D	Bray Oil Co.
		3126 Hydraulic Oil	Exxon Co. (formerly Humble Oil Co.)
		Aero Shell Fluid 4	Shell Oil Co.
		PED 3337	Standard Oil Co.
MIL-H-6083, Type I		Univis PJ-44	Exxon Oil Co. (formerly Humble Oil Co.)
		Brayco 783	Bray Oil Co.

Item 7. Battery (Nicad) - Capacity: As required

Specification	Group	Material	Manufacturer
MS36300, or		Distilled Water	Any source acceptable

  CAUTION: Before servicing, refer to paragraph 2-39.

Footnotes:

(1) Oils approved for use in Hughes 369D main transmission and tail rotor transmission are synthetic lubrication oils that have a certified Ryder Gear Value in excess of 2500 pounds.
(2) Not a preferred lubricant for Hughes 369D transmissions. Use MIL-L-7805 lubricating oil in transmissions only when other oils listed are not available.
(3) Approved for use above −40°C (−40°F).
(4) Approved for use at −54°C (−65°F) and above.
(5) For Model 250 Series engine oil change requirements and restrictions on mixing of oils, refer to Allison Commercial Service Letters.

  CAUTION: Use of mixed oils (oils meeting same specification but not in same group) in engine is permitted only in emergency and is limited to 5 hours total for each engine overhaul period.

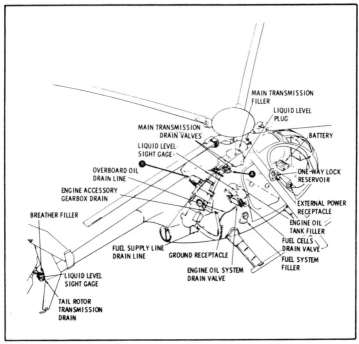

Fig. A-40. Servicing points.

Filling - Fuel System

The fuel system has two fuel cells that are interconnected for simultaneous flow and venting. Fuel system filler is on right side of helicopter.

Refuel helicopter with correct fuel as soon after landing as possible to prevent moisture condensation and to keep helicopter as heavy as possible in case of winds.

Keep fueling nozzle free of all foreign matter.

Check filler cap for security after fueling.

Draining - Fuel System

Fuel draining should be accomplished with helicopter as level as possible.

Fuel system may be defueled in two ways. One is to defuel through filler port, using a pump. The other method is to open system drain valves on fuselage underside and in engine compartment.

Fuel cells drain valve is spring-loaded closed and is opened by depressing internal plunger.

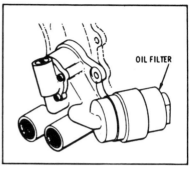

Fig. A-41. Transmission lubrication pump.

Fuel supply line drain valves are needle and seat-type, and open by counterclockwise rotation of hex fitting and attached drain line.

After defueling, be sure to close and lockwire drain valves.

Caution

To avoid possible damage to fuel pump, do not operate fuel pump with fuel tanks drained.

Filling - Engine Oil System

The engine oil tank filler is on the right side of the helicopter. A liquid level sight gauge for checking oil level in tank is visible through a transparent window near the filler.

Check oil level.

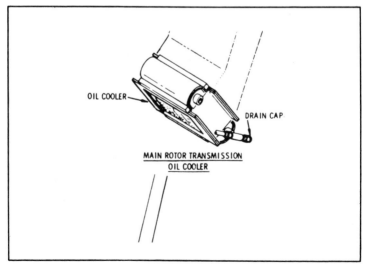

Fig. A-42. Main rotor transmission oil cooler.

Replenish with correct oil until oil level is at FULL on sight gauge.

Make certain that oil tank filler cap is securely tightened immediately after servicing.

Draining - Engine Oil System

Remove interior trim and aft bulkhead right access cover.

Place a suitable container under overboard oil drain line where it exits fuselage underside at firewall.

Remove cap from engine oil tank filler. Pull out knurled spring-loaded button to open valve in engine oil drain line just below engine oil cooler. Rotate button and valve poppet so that locking pin rests on shoulders of pin slot.

After draining oil from tank, reinstall filler cap and close oil drain valve; ensure that poppet pin is in stop slot.

Reinstall access door and interior trim.

To drain approximately ½ pint of residual oil from engine accessory gearbox drain, remove wire lead and lower chip detector. Use suitable container to catch oil. Check that detector O-ring is serviceable (replace if necessary); reinstall detector, torque to 50-60 inch-pounds and reconnect wire lead.

Filling - Main Rotor Transmission and Tail Rotor Transmission

Transmission (gearbox) oil should be replaced with new oil whenever it is drained.

Note

Replace oil pump filter after oil is drained from main transmission and at intervals specified in HMI.

Remove trim cover and check transmission oil level at liquid level sight gauge. Replenish with correct oil until oil level is at FULL on sight gauge.

Note

If oil was drained from transmission cooler: after replenishing oil ground operate helicopter for 15 minutes, then recheck oil level at liquid level sight gauge. Replenish oil as necessary. This purges air from oil cooling system and ensures that entire oil cooling system is full.

Fill main transmission by lifting breather-filler cap and inserting spout of oil can into opening. Check that spring-loaded cap closes when oil can spout is removed.

Fill tail rotor transmission by removing lockwire, unscrewing breather-filler, and pouring oil into transmission. Check that filler

O-ring is serviceable (replace if necessary). Reinstall breather-filler and torque 45-55 inch-pounds with breather hole aft at completion of torquing; secure with lockwire.

Draining - Main Transmission

Remove main transmission cooler drain cap and drain oil into suitable container.

Remove main transmission drain access covers, wire leads, and chip detectors.

Using main transmission drain hose, drain oil into suitable container.

If damaged, replace O-rings used with chip detectors and self-closing valves.

If removed, reinstall self-closing valve (50-60 inch-pounds torque) and chip detector (40-50 inch-pounds torque). Lockwire valve to gearbox and detector to valve. Reconnect wire leads.

Reinstall main transmission drain covers.

Note
Main transmission filter is to be replaced whenever oil is drained.

Draining - Tail Rotor Transmission

Position suitable container under tail rotor transmission drain.

Remove wire lead, lockwire, chip detector, and self-closing valve.

If damaged, replace O-rings used with chip detector and self-closing valve.

After oil drains, install self-closing valve (50-60 inch-pounds torque) and chip detector (40-50 inch-pounds torque). Lockwire valve to gearbox and detector to valve. Reconnect wire lead.

Wipe dry any oil spillage with clean cloth moistened with solvent.

Replacing Transmission Lubrication Pump Oil Filter

Remove interior trim and blower access door (Figs. A-43, A-44).

Position container of cloth to catch residual oil. Loosen and remove filter housing by turning counterclockwise (Figs. A-45, A-46).

Remove filter element.

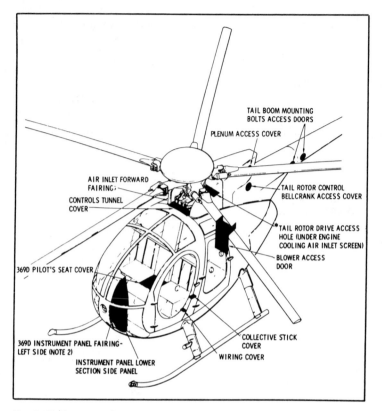

Fig. A-43. Access and inspection provisions and locations I.

Inspect filter element for metal particles. If metal particles are present, remove main transmission chip detectors and inspect for other evidence of internal failure in gear box.

Install new filter element and new O-rings.

Install and tighten housing.

If necessary, replenish transmission oil supply; then perform ground runup of helicopter and check splitline for oil leakage.

Reinstall, in order, blower access door and interior trim.

Replacing Engine Fuel Filter

Refer to *Allison Engine Operation and Maintenance Manual.*

Servicing - One-Way Lock Control System

Remove pilot's seat cover to check oil level. Reservoir should be minimum ¾ full.

If oil level in reservoir is low, lift filler cap and add oil as needed. Reinstall pilot's seat cover.

Caution

Do not fill more than ¾ full. Filling over ¾ full causes expelling of fluid if cyclic is moved forward quickly, resulting in false indication of leakage.

Note

If oil level is consistently low, one-way lock should be repaired to stop oil leakage according to instructions in 369 D - COM.

Battery Handling and Servicing Precautions

Warning

Electrolyte used in nickel-cadmium batteries contains potassium hydroxide, a caustic chemical agent. Serious burns

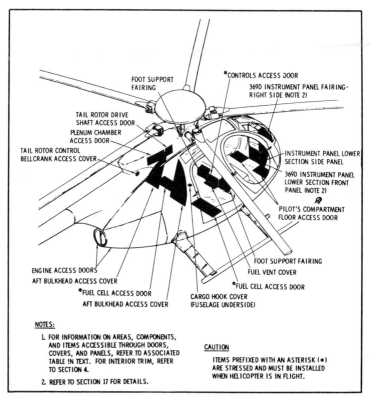

Fig. A-44. Addess and inspection provisions and locations II.

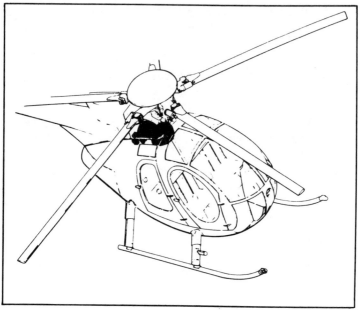

Fig. A-45. Oil filter—transmission lubrication pump I.

result if electrolyte contacts skin. Explosive gases may be released from battery during charging. Before removing battery from helicopter, make sure that power selector switch is at OFF position. Removal or installation of battery connector while battery is under load may result in explosion, electrical arcing, or possible severe burns. When charging battery, comply with procedures in following section under Battery Charging. (For battery removal and installation information, refer to HMI.)

Battery Servicing

Battery servicing consists of replenishing any electrolyte water that may have been lost through normal gassing, venting, or overcharging. Lost water should be replaced with pure distilled water only. Never use potassium hydroxide solution.

Caution

Electrolyte level should be checked only after battery has been fully charged and then allowed to rest (stand idle) for a period of one to two hours. If helicopter is operated continuously for minimum of one hour or more, battery may be considered fully charged.

Turn power selector switch OFF.

Raise pilot compartment floor left access door and remove battery cover.

Caution

Use care to avoid damaging battery temperature sensing wires, and switch connections during cleaning and servicing.

Wipe tops of cells with clean cloth and remove filler vent caps.

Check electrolyte level in each cell according to manufacturer's instructions.

Caution

Do not add distilled water if battery has remained idle for more than two hours after flight (charging). Electrolyte level will drop in a longer time interval, and any added water would result in overflowing.

Note

If electrolyte level is low to the extend that it is not visible, remove battery from helicopter for bench charging and servicing.

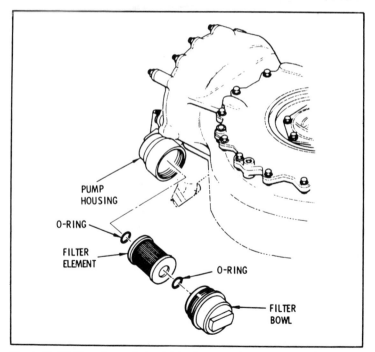

Fig. A-46. Oil filter—transmission lubrication pump II.

Using thoroughly clean bulb-type syringe that has never been used for servicing a lead-acid battery, add pure distilled water as necessary to raise electrolyte ¼-⅜ inch above plates.

If there is surplus electrolyte, replace battery; or remove battery and service in accordance with manufacturer's instructions.

Note

If battery with surplus electrolyte is serviced, it must be checked for serviceability according to manufacturer's instructions before reinstallation and reuse in helicopter.

Reinstall filler vent caps.

Reinstall battery cover, mounting screws and washers; close and latch access door.

Battery Charging

Nickel-cadmium battery charging is accomplished by either normal charging method or deep-cycling method, depending upon circumstances.

Normal battery charging consists of charging battery by constant potential method or constant current method and adjusting electrolyte level if required.

Normal battery charging is accomplished when need arises.

Deep cycling consists of intentionally discharging and then recharging battery, adjusting electrolyte level, checking battery output capability (capacity discharge test) and again recharging.

Deep cycling should be accomplished on a new battery before it is installed in helicopter, if required, and at inspection intervals specified in HMI.

Deep cycling should also be accomplished after battery repairs such as replacement of individual cells or battery case, and after any idle period of 90 days or more.

Note

Follow manufacturer's operation instructions for battery charger; however, all voltage values, discharge rates, and charging schedules given in following paragraphs shall apply in event of conflict with constant potential battery charger instructions.

Normal Charging of Battery

Warning

Review battery handling and servicing precautions outlined in previous section under Battery Servicing before performing the following charging operations.

If battery is installed in helicopter, turn power selector switch OFF and remove battery.

Clean battery.

Inspect battery for any damage that requires battery replacement or repair.

Caution

Do not add distilled water to electrolyte prior to charging, even if electrolyte is not visible. Electrolyte level will rise as charging progresses.

Charge battery as follows:

Note

The following procedures provide instructions for charging with constant potential method. When charging by constant current method, disregard procedures in the next two steps and charge battery according to battery and battery charger manufacurer's instructions. Charging is normally accomplished with cell filler vent caps installed. Temperature of battery may rise during charging.

Using constant potential charger, charge battery for 30 minutes, taking care to maintain constant and accurate charging voltage of 28.0-28.5 volts dc for full charging period.

If necessary, monitor and manually adjust charging voltage to prevent any drop or rise in charging voltage.

Switch charger OFF and then disconnect battery from charger.

Remove filler vent caps and check electrolyte level. Replenish with pure distilled water if necessary; do not overfill.

Replace and tighten filler vent caps.

Deep Cycling of Battery

Warning

Review battery handling and servicing precautions before performing the following charging operations.

Connect a 9-ohm resistance (9-ohm, 200-watt resistor or three 3-ohm, 75-watt resistors in series) across battery teminals and allow battery to discharge for approximately 12 hours, or until battery voltage decreases below 1 volt.

Remove 9-ohm load resistance from battery and loosen cell filler vent caps.

Charge battery until charging rate decreases to less than 0.03 ampere.

While continuing to charge battery at a rate less than 0.03 ampere, use an accurate voltmeter to measure voltage across terminals of each individual battery cell. Each individual cell should be within 0.5 volt of cell voltage specified below for applicable charging voltage.

Charging Voltage (volts DC)	Cell Voltage (volts DC)
28.0	1.47
28.1	1.48
28.2	1.48
28.3	1.49
28.4	1.49
28.5	1.50

Note

Nominal individual cell voltage is 1.25 volts for a normal, disconnected and fully charged cell.

Switch charger off and then disconnect battery from charger.

Allow battery to rest for minimum of one hour and maximum of two hours; adjust electrolyte level.

If electrolyte level is adjusted, reconnect battery to charger and allow battery to continue charging for 30 minutes.

Caution

If battery temperature exceeds room temperature during initial charging, battery temperature must be allowed to decrease to room temperature before recharging second time.

After allowing battery temperature to decrease to room temperature, repeat procedures described above under Deep Cycling of Battery to cycle battery a second time.

Note

When making individual voltage measurements the second time, voltage of each individual cell must measure within voltage limits specified in the fourth step described above under Deep Cycling of Battery. If voltage of any individual cell does not measure within specified voltage limits, cell must be discarded. Replace defective cell according to instructions in HMI.

Switch charger off and then disconnect battery from charger.

Tighten cell filler vent caps.

Access and Inspection Provisions

Caution

Any time maintenance work is to be performed near engine air and engine cooling air inlets, use care to prevent entry of foreign objects that might later be sucked into compressor or cooling air blower. Tape covers of cardboard or other suitable material in place over engine inlet and engine cooling air screens. Covers should not be removed until work is completed and debris is thoroughly cleaned out of the area.

Removable access doors and covers are provided in the helicopter for servicing, inspection, removal, installation, and adjustment of components.

Screws are used to secure access doors in stress areas. Liquid level sight gauges allow inspection of lubricant levels for main transmission, engine oil tank, and tail rotor transmission.

Methods for removal and installation are obvious for most doors and covers. Where necessary, instructions are provided in the following paragraphs. (For information on access doors and covers that are also used for interior trim, refer to HMI.)

Pilot Compartment Floor Access Doors

Each of the two pilot's compartment floor access doors are formed by two hinged fiberglass panels, hinged at the forward edge to the pilot's compartment floor. A latch at the rear secures each door in place. Two stainless steel heel strips are hinged and held in place over each door by a spring.

Removal - remove either floor access door as follows:

Release latch at rear of the door; raise and hold up rear of heel strips for access to hinge pin at forward end of door.

Note

Heel strips may be removed for ease of access by detaching springs from clips on underside of strips and removing hinge pins attaching forward ends of strips to antitorque pedal mounting bracket.

Remove hinge pin securing forward edge of door to pilot's compartment floor; remove door.

Installation: position door and secure forward edge to floor using hinge pin. If removed, heel strips are reinstalled by inserting hinge pins through brackets on forward end of strip and anti-torque pedal mounting bracket and connecting springs to clips on underside of heel strips.

Engine Access Doors

The two engine access doors are secured in closed position by three level-type, drawn hook latches.

Note

Do not attempt to remove hinge pivot bolts and spacers. (For disassembly at hinge points and for all door maintenance, refer to HMI.)

Removal: release three latches to open access doors. Index mark hinge, shim, and serrated plate to door structure. Remove three engine access door hinge attachment screws with washers. Forward screws are attached with nuts and aft screws attach to rivnuts.

Installation: position door and temporarily install shim, serrated plate, and attachment hardware. Align indexing marks on shim, serrated plate, and hinge with those on door and then tighten screws. Close and latch doors and check for firm fit with no deflection. (If further adjustment is required, refer to HMI.)

Cleaning

General cleaning of oil and dirt and deposits from the helicopter and its components must be accomplished by using dry-cleaning solvent, standard commercial grade kerosene, or a solution of detergent soap and water.

Exceptions that must be observed are specified in the following cleaning paragraphs.

Caution

Some commercial cleaning agents, such as readily available household cleaners, contain chemicals that can cause corrosive action and/or leave residue that can result in corrosion. Examples of cleaning agents that are *not* to be used are "Fantastic"- and "409"-type cleaners, or locally made strong soap cleaners.

Cleaning Fuselage Interior Trim and Upholstery

Clean dirt or dust accumulations from floors and other metal surfaces with vacuum cleaner or small hand brush.

Sponge soiled upholstery and trim panels with a mild soap and lukewarm water solution. Avoid complete soaking of upholstery and trim panels. Wipe solution residue from upholstery with cloth dampened with clean water.

Remove embedded grease or dirt from upholstery and carpeting by sponging or wiping with an upholstery cleaning solvent recommended for the applicable fabric (nylon, vinyl, leather, etc.).

Note

If necessary, seat upholstery may be thoroughly dry-cleaned with solvent. When complete dry-cleaning is performed, upholstery must be reflameproofed in compliance with Federal Aviation Regulation Part 27.

Cleaning Airframe Exterior and Rotor Blades

Caution

Use care to prevent scratching of aluminum skin when cleaning main rotor blades. Never use volatile solvents or abrasive materials. Never apply bending loads to blades or blade tabs during cleaning.

Wash helicopter exterior, including fiberglass components and rotor blades, when necessary, using solution of clean water and mild soap.

Note

Avoid directing soapy or clean water concentrations toward engine air intake area and instrument static source ports in aft fairing.

Clean surfaces stained with fuel or oil by wiping with soft cloth dampened by solvent, followed by washing with clean water and mild soap.

Rinse washed areas with water and dry with soft cloth.

Cleaning Transparent Plastic

Clean outside surfaces of plastic panels by rinsing with clean water and rubbing lightly with palm of hand.

Use mild soap and water solution or aircraft-type plastic cleaner to remove oil spots and similar residue.

Caution

Never attempt to dry plastic panels with cloth. To do so causes any abrasive particles lying on plastic to scratch or dull surface. Wiping with dry cloth also builds up an electro-static charge that attracts dust particles from air.

After dirt is removed from surface of plastic, rinse with clean water and let air-dry or dry with soft, damp chamois.

Clean inside surfaces of plastic panels by using aircraft-type plastic cleaner and tissue-quality paper wipers.

Cleaning Battery

Check that electrical power selector switch on instrument panel is OFF.

Unlatch and raise pilot compartment floor left access door; remove cover.

Caution

Use care to avoid damaging battery temperature sensing wires and switch connections during cleaning.

Clean battery in accordance with manufacturer's instruction manual.

Reinstall battery cover; lower and latch floor access door.

Cleaning Battery Electrolyte Spillage

Warning

Electrolyte is a strong alkaline solution and is harmful to skin and clothing. Wear protective clothing that is used exclusively for sevicing nickel-cadmium batteries. Neutralize and flush electrolyte from skin or hands as described below.

Where there is evidence of spewed or spilled battery electrolyte, flush off surface immediately with water (cold if possible) and neutralize with 3-percent boric acid solution.

Follow with thorough flushing of cleanwater (cold if possible).

Cleaning Engine Oil Filters

Refer to *Engine Operation and Maintenance Manual.*

Cleaning Engine Compressor

Clean engine compressor according to *Engine Operation and Maintenance Manual* and the following limits.

The starter-generator can be used to motor Allison 250 Series engine for compressor cleaning cycles each 50 or more hours.

Input voltage should be 24 vdc, but it is permissible to use 12 vdc.

To prevent starter-generator damage, duty cycle (cranking) time limits that must not be exceeded are:

24 Vdc External Auxiliary Power	24 Vdc Helicopter Battery Power
25 Seconds ON	40 Seconds ON
30 Seconds OFF	60 Seconds OFF
25 Seconds ON	40 Seconds ON
30 Seconds OFF	60 Seconds OFF
25 Seconds ON	40 Seconds ON
30 Minutes OFF	30 Minutes OFF

12 Vdc External Auxiliary Power

2 Minutes ON
30 Minutes OFF
2 Minutes ON

Note

Current required by starter-generator to maintain 10 percent N_1 rpm should be approximately 150 amperes with 12 vdc input.

Cleaning of Air Inlet Screens

Remove engine air inlet screen and engine cooling air screen (refer to HMI).

Clean screens with soft brush to remove dirt accumulations.

Immerse screen in solution of detergent and allow to soak approximately 15 minutes. Flush out with clear water. Allow screen to drain and air-dry thoroughly.

Fluid Leak Analysis

Main or Tail Rotor Transmission—Oil Leak: oil leakage, seepage, or capillary wetting at oil seals or assembly joint lines of main or tail rotor transmission are permissible if leakage rate does not exceed 2 cc per hour (one drop per minute). An acceptable alternate rate of leakage from either transmission is if oil loss is not more than from full to the add mark on sight gauge within 25 flight hours. (Repair leaks according to instructions in 369D - COM.)

Note

On transmission input pinion gear oil seals with less than two hours of operation, some seepage or wetting of adjacent surfaces is normal until seal is wetted and worn-in (seated). If seepage continues at rate of one drop per minute or less, seal may be continued in service. Check transmission oil level and observe seepage rate after every two hours of operation. Shorter inspection periods may be required if seal leakage appears to be increasing.

Engine Oil Leaks

Refer to *Engine Operation and Maintenance Manual* for definition of permissible engine oil leakage.

Landing Gear Damper Hydraulic Fluid Leak

Hydraulic fluid leakage from any of landing gear dampers is not permissible. If leakage is present, damper assembly should be overhauled (369D - COM) as required and serviceable unit installed. If leaking landing gear damper is not replaced when leakage is noticed, continuation of damper in service can cause internal damage that might otherwise not occur.

Note

It is normal for a thin hydraulic oil film to remain on damper piston as a result of wiping contact with piston seal. Newly installed dampers may also have slight oil seepage from oil tapped in end cap threads during damper assembly. Neither of these should be considered damper leakage or cause for damper replacement.

Overruning Clutch - Oil Leak

When oil leakage or seepage is noticed at oil seals or assembly joint lines of overruning clutch, clutch requires further inspection and investigation as follows.

Caution

Checking clutch oil level requires removal of main transmission drive shaft. Do not stress drive shaft diaphragms during shaft removal and installation. Diaphragm deflection is limited because of material hardness.

Remove trim and blower and access door. Remove bolts and washers from each end of transmission drive shaft (Fig. A-47). Carefully slide shaft from drive couplings; do not strike shaft against any object. Remove coupling bolt and O-ring from end of clutch.

Check that the three drain holes in clutch housing are clean and free of obstruction. Oil leakage may indicate engine power output seal leakage if clutch oil level is checked and within limits.

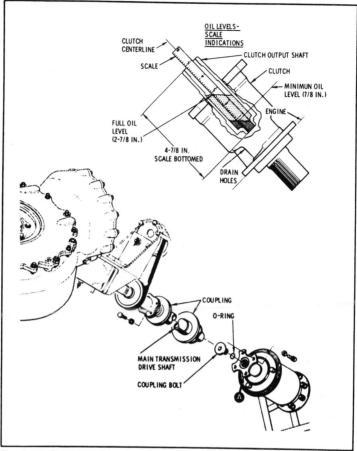

Fig. A-47. Checking oil level—overrunning clutch.

Using a *clean* 6-inch machinist's scale (½-inch width), slowly insert scale into center of clutch output shaft until scale bottoms. Scale must be inserted 4-⅞ inches.

Note

As required, trim edge of scale to reduce width of scale and allow scale to bottom in clutch.

Read scale to determine oil level and servicing required: full oil level is indicated by oil level of 2-⅞ inches on scale. Recheck reading a minimum of three times. Minimum allowable quantity (13 cc) is ⅞ inches on scale. Recheck reading a minimum of three times.

Note

If oil quantity is less than 13 cc, clutch subassembly must be removed for repair according to applicable instructions in Section 9 and 369D - COM.

Service clutch with lubricating oil (5, Table A-9) if oil level readings indicate less than full level. Do not overfill. Recheck oil level as in the steps above.

If coupling was removed, shim coupling so that there is 0.035 to 0.055 inch O-ring gap. (For clutch installation and shimming requirement details, refer to HMI.)

Caution

When installing clutch coupling bolt in the next step, installation torque on the bolt must not be less than 250 to 300 inch-pounds. Torquing to lower value reduced clutch bearing clamp-up and may result in bearing race spinning.

Coat bolt threads with oil (1, Table A-9). Install coupling bolt and O-ring. (Drag torque for bolt self-locking serviceability is 15 inch-pounds minimum, 150 inch-pounds maximum.) Torque bolt to actual drag torque plus 250 to 300 inch-pounds.

Position main transmission drive shaft between drive couplings. Install four bolts and washers and torque bolts to 50-70 inch-pounds. Reinstall blower access door and trim.

One-Way Lock - Hydraulic Fluid Leak

Hydraulic fluid leakage from any part of one-way lock is not permissible. When leakage is observed, assembly should be overhauled (369D - COM) as required and serviceable unit installed.

If leaking one-way lock is not replaced when leakage occurs, continuation in service may result in mechanical malfunction that could be hazardous to safety of flight.

Preservation and Storage

A helicopter to be placed in storage or nonoperational status must have adequate inspection, maintenance, and preservation to avoid unnecessary deterioration of airframe and components or equipment.

Extent of preventive maintenance that is to be performed depends on anticipated time in storage. The following paragraphs describe what should be performed on the helicopter for flyable storage up to 45 days.

Flyable Storage (No Time Limit)

Inspection Before Storage:

Perform Daily Inspection (HMI);

Ensure that fuel cells are full (topped off), and that oil in engine oil tank and main and tail rotor transmissions is at FULL level.

Storage: to maintain a flyable storage condition, perform daily inspection; ground runup must also be performed at least once every 7 days.

Perform Daily Inspection (HMI).

Start engine. After idle stabilizes, accelerate engine to 100 percent N_2, collective full down. Operate until oil temperature is in normal operating range and ammeter indicates battery is fully charged.

Drain fuel cell sump. (Replenish fuel as necessary.)

Ensure that fuel shutoff valve is closed.

Open movable air vents in each door of cargo compartment. Position opening in each air vent downward. Close all other vents.

Install covers and equipment used to park and moor helicopter.

Install a static ground.

Return to Service: remove covers and equipment used to park and moor helicopter; Perform Daily Inspection (HMI).

Torque Data

Torque Wrenches: Torque wrenches should be of good quality, and calibration must be verified at least every 90 days to verify accuracy.

Application of Torque Wrench Loads: Recommended tightening torque values and minimum drag torque values for fine and coarse thread nuts, and minimum breakaway torque for used self-locking bolts or screws are shown in HMI.

Appendix B

Major Helicopter Manufacturers

Bell Helicopter TEXTRON
Post Office Box 482
Fort Worth, Texas 76101
Boeing Vertol Company
Post Office Box 16858
Philadelphia, Pennsylvania 19242
The Enstrom Helicopter Corporation
Post Office Box 277
Twin County Airport
Minominee, Michigan 49857
Hiller Aviation
2075 West Scranton Avenue
Porterville, California 93257
Hughes Helicopters
Centinela and Teale Streets
Culver City, California 90230
Robinson Helicopter Company
24747 Crenshaw Boulevard
Torrance, California 90505
Spitfire Helicopter Company, Ltd.
Post Office Box 61
Media, Pennsylvania 19063

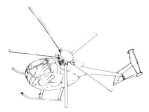

Index

254

255